W9-CMP-607

WORLD
HISTORY SERIES

Building the
Transcontinental
Railroad

Titles in the World History Series

The Age of Augustus
The Age of Exploration
The Age of Feudalism
The Age of Napoleon
The Age of Pericles
The Alamo
America in the 1960s
The American Revolution
Ancient Chinese Dynasties
Ancient Greece
The Ancient Near East
The Assyrian Empire
The Battle of the
    Little Bighorn
The Black Death
The Byzantine Empire
Caesar's Conquest of Gaul
The California Gold Rush
The Chinese Cultural
    Revolution
The Civil Rights Movement
The Collapse of the
    Roman Republic
Colonial America
The Computer Revolution
The Conquest of Mexico
The Constitution and the Founding of
    America
The Crimean War
The Cuban Missile Crisis
The Early Middle Ages
Egypt of the Pharaohs
The Enlightenment
The Great Depression
Greek and Roman
    Mythology

Greek and Roman Science
Greek and Roman Sport
Greek and Roman Theater
The History of Medicine
The History of Rock & Roll
The History of Slavery
The Incan Empire
The Italian Renaissance
The Late Middle Ages
The Making of the Atom Bomb
The Mexican-American War
The Mexican Revolution
The Mexican War of
    Independence
The Mongol Empire
The Persian Empire
Prohibition
The Punic Wars
The Reagan Years
The Reformation
The Renaissance
The Rise and Fall of the
    Soviet Union
The Roaring Twenties
Roosevelt and the
    New Deal
Russia of the Tsars
The Salem Witch Trials
The Space Race
The Spanish-American War
The Stone Age
The Titanic
Traditional Africa
Twentieth Century Science
The War of 1812

WORLD
HISTORY SERIES

Building the Transcontinental Railroad

by
James Barter

Lucent Books, P.O. Box 289011, San Diego, CA 92198-9011

Library of Congress Cataloging-in-Publication Data

Barter, James, 1946–
    Building the transcontinental railroad / by James Barter.
        p. cm. — (World history series)
    Includes bibliographical references and index.
    Summary: Discusses the history of the transcontinental
railroad, including the construction of the Central Pacific,
Union Pacific, and other related railroads which joined the
east and west coasts.
    ISBN 1-56006-880-9 (lib. : alk. paper)
    1. Pacific railroads—Juvenile literature. [1. Pacific
railroads. 2. Railroads—History.] I. Title. II. Series.
TF25 .B38 2002
385'.0973—dc21

2001001443

Contents

Foreword   6

**Important Dates in the Building of the
Transcontinental Railroad**   8

INTRODUCTION
Spanning a Vast Continent   10

CHAPTER 1
America's Will: Manifest Destiny   13

CHAPTER 2
America's Ability: The Industrial Revolution   26

CHAPTER 3
Linking East and West   39

CHAPTER 4
The Central Pacific: East Across the Sierra Nevada   52

CHAPTER 5
The Union Pacific: West Across the Great Plains   70

CHAPTER 6
The Race to Settle the New American Landscape   85

CHAPTER 7
Troubling Consequences   98

EPILOGUE
Mastering New Frontiers   112

Notes   114
For Further Reading   116
Works Consulted   118
Index   120
Picture Credits   127
About the Author   128

Foreword

Each year on the first day of school, nearly every history teacher faces the task of explaining why his or her students should study history. One logical answer to this question is that exploring what happened in our past explains how the things we often take for granted—our customs, ideas, and institutions—came to be. As statesman and historian Winston Churchill put it, "Every nation or group of nations has its own tale to tell. Knowledge of the trials and struggles is necessary to all who would comprehend the problems, perils, challenges, and opportunities which confront us today." Thus, a study of history puts modern ideas and institutions in perspective. For example, though the founders of the United States were talented and creative thinkers, they clearly did not invent the concept of democracy. Instead, they adapted some democratic ideas that had originated in ancient Greece and with which the Romans, the British, and others had experimented. An exploration of these cultures, then, reveals their very real connection to us through institutions that continue to shape our daily lives.

Another reason often given for studying history is the idea that lessons exist in the past from which contemporary societies can benefit and learn. This idea, although controversial, has always been an intriguing one for historians. Those who agree that society can benefit from the past often quote philosopher George Santayana's famous statement, "Those who cannot remember the past are condemned to repeat it." Historians who subscribe to Santayana's philosophy believe that, for example, studying the events that led up to the major world wars or other significant historical events would allow society to chart a different and more favorable course in the future.

Just as difficult as convincing students of the importance of studying history is the search for useful and interesting supplementary materials that present historical events in a context that can be easily understood. The volumes in Lucent Books' World History Series attempt to present a broad, balanced, and penetrating view of the march of history. Ancient Egypt's important wars and rulers, for example, are presented against the rich and colorful backdrop of Egyptian religious, social, and cultural developments. The series engages the reader by enhancing historical events with these cultural contexts. For example, in *Ancient Greece*, the text covers the role of women in that society. Slavery is discussed in *The Roman Empire*, as well as how slaves earned their freedom. The numerous and varied aspects of everyday life in these and other societies are explored in each volume of the series. Additionally, the series covers the major political, cultural, and philosophical ideas as the torch of civilization is passed from ancient Mesopotamia and Egypt, through Greece, Rome, Medieval Europe, and other world cultures, to the modern day.

The material in the series is formatted in a thorough, precise, and organized manner. Each volume offers the reader a comprehensive and clearly written overview of an important historical event or period. The topic under discussion is placed in a broad, historical context. For example, *The Italian Renaissance* begins with a discussion of the High Middle Ages and the loss of central control that allowed certain Italian cities to develop artistically. The book ends by looking forward to the Reformation and interpreting the societal changes that grew out of the Renaissance. Thus, students are not only involved in an historical era, but also enveloped by the events leading up to that era and the events following it.

One important and unique feature in the World History Series is the primary and secondary source quotations that richly supplement each volume. These quotes are useful in a number of ways. First, they allow students access to sources they would not normally be exposed to because of the difficulty and obscurity of the original source. The quotations range from interesting anecdotes to farsighted cultural perspectives and are drawn from historical witnesses both past and present. Second, the quotes demonstrate how and where historians themselves derive their information on the past as they strive to reach a consensus on historical events. Lastly, all of the quotes are footnoted, familiarizing students with the citation process and allowing them to verify quotes and/or look up the original source if the quote piques their interest.

Finally, the books in the World History Series provide a detailed launching point for further research. Each book contains a bibliography specifically geared toward student research. A second, annotated bibliography introduces students to all the sources the author consulted when compiling the book. A chronology of important dates gives students an overview, at a glance, of the topic covered. Where applicable, a glossary of terms is included.

In short, the series is designed not only to acquaint readers with the basics of history, but also to make them aware that their lives are a part of an ongoing human saga. Perhaps then they will come to the same realization as famed historian Arnold Toynbee. In his monumental work, *A Study of History*, he wrote about becoming aware of history flowing through him in a mighty current, and of his own life "welling like a wave in the flow of this vast tide."

IMPORTANT DATES IN THE BUILDING OF THE TRANSCONTINENTAL RAILROAD

January 1863
The Central Pacific's groundbreaking ceremonies take place at Sacramento.

1811
Work begins on the Cumberland Road, America's first public road authorized by Congress in 1806.

October 1863
The Central Pacific spikes the first rails.

June 1861
The Big Four and Theodore Judah incorporate the Central Pacific Railroad.

1800	1830	1850	1860	1862	1864

1819
The first section of the Erie Canal opens.

1853
Secretary of War Jefferson Davis authorizes survey parties from the Army Corps of Engineers to explore the five best rail routes to the Pacific Ocean.

July 1862
President Lincoln signs the Railroad Act, authorizing the construction of the transcontinental railroad.

1830
The first railroad in America, the Baltimore & Ohio, opens thirteen miles of track for service.

November 1863
Judah dies, leaving control of the Central Pacific to the Big Four.

December 1863
The Union Pacific's groundbreaking ceremonies take place at Council Bluffs.

January 1865
The first Chinese are hired by the Central Pacific.

November 1866
The Central Pacific begins blasting Tunnel Number 6, Summit Tunnel.

April 1868
The Union Pacific conquers Sherman Summit, Wyoming.

May 10, 1869
The official ceremony celebrating the completion of the transcontinental railroad takes place at Promontory Summit.

1887
Congress passes the Interstate Commerce Act to regulate the railroads because of their unfair treatment of farmers.

1864	1866	1868	1870	1880	1890

July 1865
The Union Pacific spikes the first rails.

November 1867
The Union Pacific reaches Cheyenne, Wyoming.

December 1867
The Central Pacific completes track acrosss the Sierra Nevada summit through Tunnel Number 6.

1872
The Crédit Mobilier scandal is exposed.

1884
Several transcontinental railroads connect eastern states with states along the Pacific coast.

July 1864
President Lincoln signs the second Railroad Act, authorizing the railroads to sell their own bonds and establishing general building limits for each railroad.

Spanning a Vast Continent

The construction of the transcontinental railroad was America's most significant engineering feat of the nineteenth century. For the first time in the history of any large nation, a railroad could reliably transport passengers and freight products from one end of the country to the other. The completion of the transcontinental railroad played a significant role in elevating America from a fledgling democracy struggling to secure its own borders to a leading industrial and economic power.

Before the completion of the transcontinental railroad, persons traveling from towns along the Missouri River to California risked their lives on a months-long journey on foot, on horseback, or by covered wagon. Crossing the two-thousand-mile expanse referred to as the Great American Desert, most of which was not yet part of the United States, was done at considerable peril. The scorching heat of the deserts and the freezing winter snows of the Sierra Nevada killed hundreds. Indian raids were a possibility on the Great Plains, and although casualties among the Indians were greater than those the Indians inflicted, the prospect of being killed

and scalped filled most pioneers with fear. In the face of such risks, many Americans preferred to take their chances on shipboard passage around the tip of South America or a sea-land-sea route via the Isthmus of Panama. Most of these travelers, however, fared no better than their compatriots in covered wagons.

Given the vastness of the North American continent, Americans early on sensed a need for faster travel between the Atlantic and Pacific Coasts. For some, connecting the East and West represented the culmination of an American dream to create an American empire secure from foreign threats. For others, that connection represented unlimited access to natural resources and endless opportunity. Regardless of why Americans wanted to create the link between the two coasts, nearly everyone believed that Americans had a right to accomplish it.

The railroad that ultimately ran between Omaha, Nebraska, and Sacramento, California, consumed unprecedented amounts of natural resources. Construction workers cut down entire forests to provide wood for railroad ties, wood to fuel locomotives, and heavy wood beams to build dozens of trestles across rivers. Iron mills along the East Coast operated around the clock to produce 200,000 tons of rails, 550 tons of spikes, and thousands of tons of assorted hardware to hold the rails together. The amount of black powder used to blast tunnels through the granite of the Sierra Nevada in California exceeded the amount used in the Civil War.

OPENING LAND FOR SETTLEMENT

The completion of the transcontinental railroad opened huge tracts of land for settlement and brought a flood of Americans to the territory between the Missouri River and the Pacific Ocean. A surge of European immigrants seeking relief from the social and economic ills at home quickly joined the Americans. As these immigrant farmers and ranchers settled the vast landscape, they planted crops and raised cattle. Before long, American farmers were producing more food than the American population could consume.

The success of the railroad came at a high cost for some Americans, however.

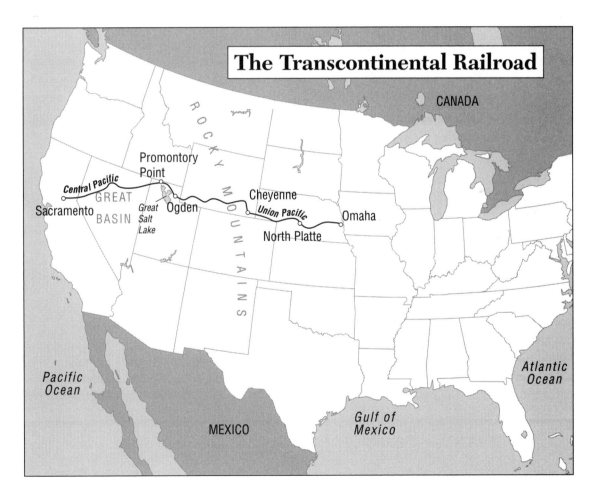

The Transcontinental Railroad

As settlers arrived following the railroad's completion, Native Americans were forced to give up their land. Many farmers and ranchers, who had once benefited from the presence of the railroads, eventually found themselves being squeezed out of business by the high freight charges the railroad levied.

No matter how historians evaluate its legacy, however, nearly all agree that few engineering undertakings have had as significant an impact on the development of the nation as the transcontinental railroad did. The building of the transcontinental railroad, then, is a story that deserves telling.

Chapter

1 America's Will: Manifest Destiny

Acquiring land was one of the major reasons the early seventeenth-century colonists abandoned Europe in search of new lives in America. Upon their arrival in North America, the English and Dutch cleared land for farms and established small towns, and as more settlers arrived, they expanded north and south along the Atlantic coast. By the early eighteenth century, the thirteen original colonies were brimming with farmers and small businesses. By the middle of the eighteenth century, several major cities, such as Boston, Philadelphia, Baltimore, and New York, teemed with commercial activity. Although the population of the thirteen colonies was only about one and one-half million, many colonists felt the need to find new lands farther from the growing population centers.

The first Europeans to land in the New World early in the seventeenth century had found what seemed to them limitless amounts of land. Yet, in less than 150 years, Americans living along the East Coast began looking to the west to satisfy their need for open space. Mountain men and fur traders were eager to see what lay beyond the Appalachian mountain range

that extended from Maine to Georgia. These early trailblazers who ventured into this vast wilderness to the west returned telling colorful stories of boundless plains and valleys with soil so rich that scattered seeds quickly grew, and of forests so plentiful with wild game that a single musket shot would drop two animals.

Stories such as these, often more fanciful than accurate, fueled the imagination of many early settlers wanting to move west. Before the founding of the United States in 1776, an estimated ten thousand Americans had already moved west along the Ohio River as far as the tiny settlement that would one day become known as Pittsburgh. By the early 1780s, another fifty thousand settlers, led by Daniel Boone and other frontiersmen, had pushed through the Cumberland Gap into the Kentucky and Tennessee territories. Britain's claim to this territory did not deter Americans from settling there, since these early immigrants believed that unoccupied land was theirs for the taking.

In 1783, in the treaty ending the Revolutionary War, the British relinquished rights to all land between the Appalachians and the Mississippi River. This addition of territory quadrupled the size of the new nation and encouraged even more settlers to move west. By the end of the eighteenth century, tens of thousands of Americans—mostly farmers and trappers—had arrived in the territory only sparsely populated by Native American tribes.

The acquisition of land for farming was also given a boost by Thomas Jefferson, who imparted a moral tone to its importance. In 1787, Jefferson wrote of the importance of working the land:

> Those who labour in the earth are the chosen people of God, if ever he had a chosen people, whose beasts he has made his peculear deposit for substantial and genuine virtue. . . . While we have land to labour then, let us never wish to see our citizens occupied at a workbench, or twirling a distaff [a wooden staff used in spinning wool] . . . for the general operations of manufacture, let our workshops remain in Europe.[1]

MORE LAND

But even the vast tracts of land between the Appalachians and the Mississippi River were insufficient for Americans. Harriet Martineau, an Englishwoman ob-

Settlers on the East Coast were eager to see the land to the west, beyond the Appalachian Mountains.

THE OHIO VALLEY

The pioneers who first settled the Ohio Valley did so without legal authorization. The British had taken control of this area from the French in 1763 and controlled it until 1776, when they lost it to the Americans following the Revolutionary War. However, before the young American government in Philadelphia could organize, thousands of settlers moved into the valley, taking tracts of land without purchasing them and without holding title. David Colbert, in his book Eyewitness to the American West, *quotes one such settler and veteran of the Revolutionary War, John May, who describes his travels in the Ohio Valley, the Indians, and the hardships in 1788.*

"Thursday, [May] 29th. I was engaged this afternoon with the surveyors. Found the soil very good but was tormented beyond measure by myriads [thousands] of gnats. They not only bit tremendously, but get down one's throat.

This evening, arrived two long boats from the Rapids, with officers and soldiers, the number about one hundred. On their passage up the river they were fired upon by a Strobridge party of Indians, headed by a white man. They returned the fire, and had two men killed. They were obliged to drop down the river a piece, and come by the place in the night. There are various reports about the hostility of the savages, but nothing to be depended on. The Indians are frequently in here, and seem to be on friendly terms. I have shaken hands with many of them.

Sunday, [May] 17th. A number of poor devils— five in all—took their departure homeward this morning. They came from home moneyless and brainless, and have returned as they came."

serving this phenomenon late in the eighteenth century, wrote:

> The pride and delight of Americans, is in their quantity of land. I do not remember meeting with one to whom it had occurred that they had too much. . . . The possession of land is the aim of all action . . . and the cure for all social evils. . . . If a man is disappointed in politics or love, he goes and buys more land. If he disgraces himself, he betakes himself to a lot in the West.[2]

Before long, Americans began pressing still farther west, this time into territory claimed by France and known as Louisiana. Just as they had in British territory earlier, Americans settled in Louisiana with the belief that they had the right to claim seemingly unoccupied land.

Louisiana, as it turned out, was not destined to remain in French hands for

LEWIS AND CLARK EXPEDITION

In 1804, President Thomas Jefferson ordered Meriwether Lewis and William Clark to assemble an expedition to explore the vast, new territory the United States had just purchased from France. Returning to St. Louis two years later after traversing eight thousand miles, they reported to Jefferson the rich bounty of natural resources they had witnessed. In this excerpt, which appears in David Colbert's, Eyewitness to the American West, *Lewis describes the discovery of the source of the Missouri River. Descriptions such as this inspired the need to protect this territory from rival countries and fueled America's sense of manifest destiny.*

"At a distance of 4 miles further the road took us to the most distant fountain of the waters of the Mighty Missouri in search of which we have spent so many toilsome days and restless nights. Thus far I had accomplished one of those great objectives on which my mind has been unalterably fixed for many years, judge then of the pleasure I felt allaying my thirst with this pure and ice-cold water. . . . After refreshing ourselves, we proceeded on to the top of the dividing ridges from which I discovered immense ridges of high mountains still to the west of us with their tops partially covered with snow."

Meriwether Lewis (pictured) and William Clark explored Louisiana and other areas around the Mississippi River that the United States had purchased from France.

long. In 1803, President Jefferson and Congress recognized the value of adding this huge tract of land to the nation and purchased it from France for $15 million. This acquisition became known as the Louisiana Purchase, and it added eight hundred thousand square miles of land to the United States, doubling its size. The territory encompassed by the Louisiana Purchase was so large and mysterious that President Jefferson ordered a party headed by Meriwether Lewis and William Clark to explore and map it and chronicle their findings.

In 1804, Lewis and Clark began their explorations from St. Louis. They followed the Missouri River northwest. Moving well beyond the agreed-upon boundary of Louisiana, in 1805 they crossed through parts of Oregon and Washington along the Snake and Columbia Rivers, eventually arriving at the shore of the Pacific Ocean. Lewis and Clark's stories of fertile valleys, rivers with an abundance of fish, and seemingly endless stands of timber stirred their listeners with visions of boundless opportunities. The Louisiana Purchase made America significantly larger than any western European nation, yet relatively little of that land was actually settled at first. Lewis and Clark's report of untouched land in the valleys of what is today Oregon and Washington, coupled with similar stories told by trappers and hunters, attracted pioneers willing to take their chances on the two-thousand-mile trek from America's western-most settlements along the Mississippi River to the Pacific Coast in covered wagons.

WHO OWNED THE LAND?

In their enthusiasm to settle land, Americans continued to overlook the question of who really owned that land. Although the British and French had claimed ownership of large portions of the continent, those claims were largely based on a misunderstanding between the Europeans and the Native Americans. Initially the Indians traded their hunting grounds in exchange for inexpensive trinkets that Europeans offered. In part, this was because the Indians did not conceive of land ownership in the same way Europeans did. At first, the Indians did not fully realize that when they traded or sold their land, they had to leave and never return. As the eighteenth century moved forward, the Indians realized their mistake and began to refuse to sell or trade away any more territory. White settlers' response to this refusal was to simply take the land by force.

For Indians living in the path of the whites' westward expansion, the American dream of acquiring and farming property was a nightmare. As settlers headed west, they pushed the Indians aside. Initially the U.S. government drew up treaties offering Native Americans lands well to the west in exchange for the territory they currently occupied. Some tribes signed the treaties to avoid warfare with the whites. Others fought to keep their lands, and only after bloody battles did they agree to move. By the end of the eighteenth century, many of the Indians living on the East Coast had been forced to move west across the Mississippi River.

Native Americans found they could not prevent settlers from moving onto the land, and after many bloody battles, agreed to move to an area sanctioned as Indian Territory.

THE INDIAN PROBLEM

The territories that the U. S. government set aside for these Indians from the eastern states were so remote that it seemed few whites would ever have any use for them. In 1830, Congress passed the Indian Removal Act, which gave the American president the authority to remove Indians living in areas of the eastern United States to an area called Indian Territory.

The question of who had the right to the land was brushed aside by the excitement of settlers moving west and was never seriously debated in Congress. Settlers wanted the land, and Congress was willing to defend their right to take it. In a relatively short period, it was evident to everyone including the Indians that the migration west would continue.

MANIFEST DESTINY

As settlers gradually moved west, they left small towns in their wake. For most Americans, these small towns, with their schools, churches, and small businesses, represented civilization. The federal government's policies reflected this idea as well. The general feeling throughout the nation was that the clearing of the wilderness to make way for farms and towns was inevitable. Moreover, Americans believed they had a God-given mandate to be the ones to accomplish this task.

In 1845, many years after the westward movement had begun, an American journalist named John L. Sullivan observed the excitement surrounding the flood of Americans moving farther west and building their homes and communities in the new territories. He declared in a deeply patriotic magazine article that claiming all of this land was "the fulfillment of our manifest destiny to overspread the continent allotted by Providence [God] for the free development of our expanding millions."[3] The notion of manifest destiny struck a chord throughout America, and the term appeared in other magazines and newspapers across the country. In the eyes of many settlers and entrepreneurs, manifest

INDIANS VERSUS THE UNITED STATES SUPREME COURT

In 1831, attorneys representing the Cherokee tribe petitioned the U.S. Supreme Court to prevent the state of Georgia from applying the Indian Removal Act. Attorneys argued that this act would cause the annihilation of the Cherokee. They further argued that previous treaties with the United States guaranteed their rights to land in Georgia. Although Chief Justice John Marshall clearly states an understanding of the Cherokee's sad dilemma, he nonetheless denied their request. Chief Justice Marshall wrote this majority opinion for the Supreme Court.

"If courts were permitted to indulge their [the Cherokee] sympathies, a case better calculated to excite them can scarcely be imagined. A people once numerous, powerful, and truly independent, found by our ancestors in the quiet and uncontrolled possession of an ample domain, gradually sinking beneath our superior policy, our arts and our arms, have yielded their lands by successive treaties, each of which contains a solemn guarantee of the residue, until they retain no more of their formerly extensive territory than is deemed necessary to their comfortable subsistence.

If it be true that the Cherokee nation have rights, this is not the tribunal [court] in which those rights are to be asserted. If it be true that wrongs have been inflicted, and that still greater are to be apprehended, this is not the tribunal which can redress the past or prevent the future."

destiny justified the taking of land whether it belonged to them or not.

Among some politicians, the notion of manifest destiny took on a tone of cultural and racial superiority. In April 1857, Caleb Cushing, a Massachusetts legislator, expressing his view of manifest destiny, derided many already living in the path of westward expansion:

> In our conquest of nature with our stalwart arms and with our dauntless hearts to back them, it happens that men, nations, races, may, must, will perish before us. That is inevitable. . . . The tribes of Indians who hunted over the land without occupying it, retire before us like the hunted deer and the buffalo themselves, deeper and deeper into the innermost recesses of the continent. And the Hispano-Americans, wasting away by apparent incapacity of self-government, are suffering one province after another to relapse into pristine desolation, and thus to be-

Because of the idea of manifest destiny, many Americans were inspired to move to the western territories, especially Texas and California.

come prepared to receive the people and the laws of the United States.[4]

Manifest destiny drove Americans to continue the western expansion. Pushing America's boundaries south to the Rio Grande in Texas also seemed reasonable. Letters about the Mexican territory known as Texas, written by Moses Austin and his son Steven, attracted thousands to settle there, despite well-documented claims to that land by the Mexican government.

CALIFORNIA: THE FINAL FRONTIER

Texas was not the only territory Americans were eyeing. Still under foreign ownership were the territories of California and Oregon, which at the time included territory that would later become the states of Oregon and Washington. Mexico owned California, while Britain laid claim to Oregon. Eventually, Mexico would be forced to cede California following the Mexican-American War; Britain by that time had already agreed to turn over Oregon to the United States.

Of the Pacific Coast territories, California was the jewel that settlers wanted because of its natural harbors, rich agriculture, temperate climate, and abundant timber. American writer Richard Henry Dana played an instrumental role in spreading the news of California's bounty in 1840 when he visited the territory and wrote of it in his novel, *Two Years Before the Mast*. Even though his was a work of fic-

tion, Dana's description of California was largely accurate:

> [California is] a country embracing four or five hundred miles of sea-coast, with several good harbors, with fine forests in the north; waters filled with fish, and the plains covered with thousands of herds of cattle; blessed with a climate, than which there can be no better in the world . . . and with a soil in which corn yields from seventy to eighty-fold.[5]

California's many known natural resources gained one more in 1848 when gold was discovered. Miners by the thousands flooded into northern California to stake their claims in the gold fields. Of all of the westward destinations, none could compete with the magnetism of San Francisco and the gold country. Capturing California became the key step in achieving America's manifest destiny.

Making California a part of America was one thing; linking California in a practical sense to the rest of the nation was another. California's isolation from the east was more extreme than that of Oregon because of the Sierra Nevada. This mountain range extends nearly the entire length of California, and most of it rises six thousand to twelve thousand feet, with several peaks above fourteen thousand feet, which created a formidable barrier to settlers. The Sierra Nevada became a death trap to many early pioneers who lost their way and got caught by the heavy winter snows.

Given such an imposing barrier, getting to California was a test of endurance

A miner pans for gold, the most valuable of natural resources discovered in California. Thousands of miners traveled to California to claim their fortunes.

and toughness. The distances were great, the travel time long, and the many other obstacles daunting. Travelers in the east had three options for reaching the West Coast: crossing two thousand miles of wilderness on horseback or covered wagon, sailing ships around the tip of South America, or the combination of two ocean voyages punctuated by cross-

ing the Isthmus of Panama on foot or by canoe.

TRAVELING TO CALIFORNIA

Heading for California by one of several overland routes was the most common and cheapest option, but the disadvantages were obvious. Would-be travelers knew that the trip from Missouri to San Francisco would take six months, if they made it at all. Indian attacks, thirst, disease, and exposure killed many. A slightly safer and more comfortable route was across the Isthmus of Panama.

Crossing the Isthmus of Panama, however, had its share of misery. Most travelers took a schooner from one of the East Coast cities down to the Panamanian port of Limón. Upon their arrival, all passengers either transferred to canoes and paddled along rivers across the forty-mile-wide isthmus, or they traversed the dense jungle to Panama's west coast in horse-drawn coaches, on burros, or on foot. Travelers who made the trip across the rain-soaked and insect-in-

fested isthmus described it as one of the most miserable experiences of their lives. The trip took three days and nights by canoe, during which time sleep was impossible, thanks to the heat, humidity, and buzzing insects. Those who walked or rode on burros suffered even more because of the slower pace and greater physical exertion. No matter how travelers chose to make the journey, tropical diseases such as dysentery, yellow fever, and malaria sickened and killed many.

Upon arriving at the Pacific port of Panama City, those who wished to book passage on a ship north to San Francisco needed to be wily negotiators. Unscrupulous captains often forced voyagers to pay dearly for the second half of the trip,

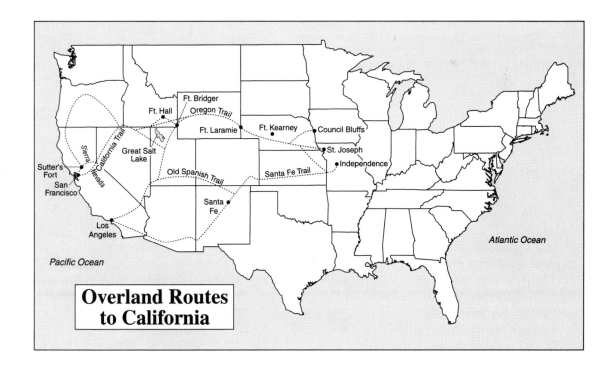

Overland Routes to California

and it made no difference whether travelers were headed east or west. Passengers were frequently stranded for a month or more while trying to arrange passage. Once passage was arranged, sometimes the advantage of the shortcut was made moot by the death of the traveler aboard ship. In 1852, for example, the passenger steamer *Philadelphia*, bound from Panama to New York, lost one-third of its passengers to cholera.

Despite the risks, plenty of Americans braved the rigors of this route to the West Coast. From 1848 to 1869, more than 375,000 Americans crossed Panama bound for California and the Northwest. During this same period, 225,000 traveled in the opposite direction.

Those who had money and time took sailing ships around Cape Horn, at the southern tip of South America. Accommodations on the eighteen-thousand-mile, six-month journey were more luxurious than those offered on the other routes. Nonetheless, passengers were guaranteed high seas that prevented them from keeping down many of their meals. Nor was the journey risk-free.

This poster advertises a ship bound for California. Instead of crossing America by land, a person could reach California by taking a ship from the East Coast to Panama, then from Panama to San Francisco.

The winds at Cape Horn were known as a tough test of the soundness of a sailing ship and the skill of its crew, and many were lost grounded on the rocks. Moreover, the one-way ticket for this tedious and dangerous passage generally cost about one thousand dollars—an amount out of reach for all but the wealthiest travelers.

The numbers of people willing to risk their lives to get to California was a testimony to the importance of linking the eastern part of the nation with the West Coast. The idea of a railroad that could provide fast, cheap, and safe travel between the two coasts had been considered, but at the same time such an extraordinary engineering challenge was insurmountable.

2 America's Ability: The Industrial Revolution

For Americans in the mid–nineteenth century, transportation problems were nothing new. From the time before the Revolutionary War, roads and trails had at least linked the original thirteen colonies together, guaranteeing their survival. Following the Revolutionary War, transportation became increasingly important for commerce between the growing cities along the East Coast. As the new nation expanded westward, transportation needs grew as well, but the means of transportation remained virtually unchanged: horse-drawn coaches, horseback, or on foot.

EARLY AMERICAN TRANSPORTATION

For Americans at the time, the main problem was the time it took to make a journey of any distance, because of the roughness of the terrain. Few roads wide enough to accommodate carriages or wagons had been cut through the dense forests of the Northeast. The 190-mile trip from New York to Boston was a seven-day trip by horse—even in good weather—and nearly twice as long on foot. Eventually, existing trails were widened, and logs laid side by

Horse-drawn coaches were used to travel America's rough roads.

side across the trails provided a firm road-head. Coaches traveling these so-called corduroy or washboard roads were less apt to become mired in mud, but passengers' rides were almost unbearably rough. A British visitor named Margaret Hall wrote home in 1827 about her travel experiences in a coach:

> We jolted up here [New York] yesterday at the rate of four hours to thirteen miles and quite fast enough for the safe of one's bones, for such a road for ruts and hoes and all manner of conveniences for shaking poor mortals to pieces I have not traveled over since I crossed the Pyrenees. . . . And away we went bumping, thumping, jolting, shaking, tossing and tumbling over the wickedest road, I do think, that ever wheel rumbled upon.[6]

In 1806, Congress authorized the building of the first national road, called the Cumberland Road, which ran the eight hundred miles from Cumberland, Maryland, to Vandalia, Illinois. The road, which later became known as the National Road, had first been suggested by both Presidents George Washington and Thomas Jefferson to aid western expansion and national unity. Work began in 1811 and opened seven years later when the stretch between Cumberland and Wheeling, West Virginia, was completed. By 1838, the road extended to Springfield, Ohio, and part of the way to Vandalia, Illinois.

The Cumberland Road was the nation's first thoroughfare that was built to specific engineering requirements. Plans called for the roadway to be twenty feet wide and to have a roadbed constructed of stone eighteen inches deep at the center and twelve inches deep at the sides. Specifications even detailed the size of the stones to be used in constructing the roadbed. In addition, the plans called for a sixty-six-foot right-of-way to be cleared the entire length of the road.

As the quality and size of roads improved, larger vehicles became practical. The favorite wagon for hauling freight was the Conestoga wagon, which was capable of holding up to seven tons of freight. Drawn by six draft horses, this wagon was a rectangular wooden box mounted on four wheels and covered with a heavy tarp to protect its contents from rain. The Conestoga wagon was particularly useful when fording rivers was necessary, because the box could be removed from the wheels and floated across.

Although roads provided a vital link between big cities and new rural settlements spreading across the American frontier, the costs of wagon travel were high, roads were rough, and the speed was slow. Muddy in the winter, badly rutted in the summer, and congested year-round, most of these roads clearly had serious limitations, which became more severe as traffic increased.

To move people comfortably and freight more effectively than wagons could, visionaries suggested connecting the cities and towns in the eastern United States with a network of overland canals, which were simply large ditches dug between lakes and rivers and filled with water. These canals, they reasoned, could then be used as waterways on which flat-bottom boats could more efficiently move freight and passengers.

Some of these canals were sophisticated feats of engineering. Perhaps the best-known canal connected Buffalo, New York, on Lake Erie, with Albany, New York, on the Hudson River. Named the Erie Canal, it was 340 miles long, about 40 feet wide, and 4 feet deep. On both sides of the canal, 10-foot-wide dirt towpaths provided room for horses and mules to tow the boats. Part of the engineering difficulty the builders of the Erie Canal faced was the need to traverse terrain that was anything but level. To accomplish this feat, engineers designed eighty-three locks to raise and lower boats as the elevation of the land rose and fell.

Once the Erie Canal was finished, teams of horses towed the flat-bottom boats full of passengers and freight between Albany and Buffalo about seven miles an hour, allowing them to complete the trip in the remarkably short time of three and one-half days. Once goods reached the Hudson River, ships carried them the rest of the way to New York City. The Erie Canal provided cheaper, safer, and faster transportation for freight that formerly either traveled overland or had been sent down the Mississippi to New Orleans and then shipped up the Atlantic coast to New York.

Although initially designed to haul freight, the smooth-gliding canal boats gradually attracted many passengers. Called packet boats, these conveyances offered comfort and luxury to nineteenth-century travelers:

> "Everything on the Canal is life and motion," wrote a Boston man in 1846. "A packet has just passed filled with passengers and a man playing the

The Conestoga wagon was the preferred method of hauling freight. It was drawn by six horses that could carry up to seven tons of goods and supplies.

The Erie Canal, shown in this present-day photo, was a safe, cheap transportation route to New York City.

viol and Gentlemen and Ladies dancing." As the roof was used as a deck, the inside of the packet boats was lined with cushioned benches. Eating tables stood in the center. At night, the boat was divided into men's and women's sides by a screen or drop curtain; the benches became beds and overhead hammocks could be pulled down for braver passengers.[7]

The elaborate system of canals that flourished throughout the Northeast from 1810 to 1840 had been an exceptional improvement over the dirt roads. Still, the continued growth and expansion of factories and the migration of thousands of settlers to the West demanded even better solutions to America's transportation problems. The time had finally arrived to turn to new technologies for solutions.

THE AMERICAN INDUSTRIAL REVOLUTION

Few, if any, Americans at the time foresaw that the answer to America's transportation problems lay in a series of events known to modern historians as the industrial revolution. In the mid-1700s, England's entire economy was radically changed when inventions such as the steam engine made it possible to significantly increase the speed with which products could be manufactured. Steam engines not only drove the machinery that manufactured products such as textiles, but also provided the power to bring raw materials to the factories.

Prominent Americans visiting England saw these technological wonders and realized their potential to power a similar revolution at home. England, however,

EDUCATION

The first step on the road to the American industrial revolution was the need to create an educational system capable of training the engineers needed to invent and create machinery. Americans would need to learn all of the mathematics, physics, chemistry, and engineering principles that the British employed for their industrial revolution.

Education during the colonial period was the responsibility of local communities and churches. All schools were private and were available only to the relatively small percentage of the population that could afford the tuition. Because of this situation, there was a shortage of trained, educated people capable of providing the solutions to early nineteenth-century industrial progress.

Beginning in the 1820s, however, the need to educate more of the population became evident if America was to meet the growing challenges of an expanding nation. The influx of immigrants from Europe, combined with the westward movement, created pressure to build cities, engineer roads and canals, build machines to increase food production, and provide better health care. More people needed to have a good technical education. American educators such as Horace Mann and Henry Barnard worked to open education to the public. Although several great universities existed at the beginning of the nineteenth century, many more were needed to train the teachers, engineers, lawyers, and doctors who would provide the skills to make America's manifest destiny a reality.

America created engineering schools that based problem solving on science rather than on guesswork, as had often been the case previously. In 1822, the Lyceum opened as America's first technical school that specialized in teaching farmers scientific approaches to planting and fertilizing crops. The school also provided technical training in farm machinery operation. Two years later, the Rensselaer Polytechnic Institute opened engineering classes for the civil engineers needed to build America's roads, bridges, canals, and railroads. West Point, America's first service academy, was founded as an engineering college. By the middle of the nineteenth century, an impressive number of technical schools were providing the scientific leadership necessary to solve most of the problems of an expanding and growing population.

did not intend to share the new technology with the Americans. The British passed laws prohibiting the export of both machinery and detailed drawings of machines. Even the emigration of engineers who might share their knowledge of such machines was prohibited. England was making huge profits exporting manufactured goods to America and would lose money if Americans had the machinery to make them for themselves. Faced with England's refusal to export technology, Americans would have to develop much of their technology themselves. In small increments, Americans developed the means to fulfill their manifest destiny.

HOMEGROWN TECHNOLOGY

The American textile and milling industries were the first to benefit from homegrown technology, and both did so because of one inventor, Oliver Evans. In 1775, Evans watched workers making the cards used in the textile industry to smooth cotton and wool before it was spun into thread for clothing. The cards were similar in design to hairbrushes except that the bristles were short, sharp pieces of wire. Setting the pieces of wire by hand was a painful process resulting in many skin punctures (and serious, even deadly infections) for the workers. Evans devised a machine that set the wires faster and more accurately than they could be set manually. This first machine was relatively simple, but the next device Evans created was more sophisticated.

Evans observed the milling of flour and believed that he could build a machine capable of performing the six separate tasks that workers were doing by hand. Using his engineering skills, Evans designed a series of pulleys, gears, and buckets connected to a waterwheel. As the waterwheel turned, a conveyor belt carried the wheat to a bin and dropped it into a chute, where it was ground, cleaned, and bagged, and the bags deposited into a cart. Exact copies of this first factory mill spread throughout America.

Evans went on to realize that some factories would have to be built away from water sources that powered the early mills, noting, "Water-falls are not at our command in all places, and are liable to be obstructed by frost, drought, and any other accidents. Wind is inconstant and unsteady: animal power, expensive, tedious in the operation, and unprofitable, as well as subject to innumerable accidents."[8] So Evans designed an engine that he promised would be able to perform these functions:

> To chop grain and pump for distilleries and breweries, a very small engine will answer. . . . In paper-mills the steam engine may be employed with peculiar advantage; the *power* to cut, clean and grind the rags and work the screws of the presses; and the *steam* to heat the vats. For turning-lathes and grind-stones, a very small and cheap engine will answer.[9]

Many other industries quickly followed the textile and milling trades in replacing manual laborers with machinery.

"Who Made That Plow?"

Many of America's great manufacturers owe part of their success to the railroads. Inventions of heavy farm equipment succeeded not only because of their value to farmers but also because railroads could transport this equippment over great distances at a low cost to thousands of farmers across the country. The midwestern soil was rich, but the sod was so dense and sticky that farmers plowing their fields had to stop every few yards to knock soil clumps off their wooden plow blades. According to David Colbert in his book, Eyewitness to the American West, *an Illinois blacksmith, John Deere, got an idea while sharpening a saw blade. Believing the sticky soil might not stick to steel, he told this story to his friend Frank Kern in 1837. Within ten years of this discovery, John Deere was producing and shipping one thousand plows a year, and by 1857 that number rose to ten thousand a year. Today, the John Deere Company continues to ship most of its heavy equipment by rail and is the largest manufacturer of farm equipment in America.*

"I cut the teeth off [some circular saw blades] with a hand chisel . . . then laid them on the fire of a forge and heated what little I could at a time and shaped them as best I could with the hand hammer. I . . . finally succeeded in constructing a very rough plow. I set it on a box by the side of the shop-door. A few days after, a farmer from across the river drove up. Seeing the plow, he asked:

'Who made that plow?'

'I did, such as it is, wood work and all.'

'Hell,' said the farmer, 'that looks like it would work. Let me take it home and try it, and if it works all right, I'll keep it and pay you for it. If not I will return it.'

'Take it,' said I, 'and give it a thorough trial.'

About two weeks later, the farmer drove up to the shop, without the plow, and paid for it, and said: 'Now get a move on and make me two more plows just like the other one.'"

Inventors quickly realized that any industry requiring simple, repeatable tasks such as drilling or crushing could benefit from specialized machinery. In 1760 in New York City, Pierre Lorillard built the first tobacco factory that used mills to crush and then cut tobacco leaves into short strands for pipe tobacco and into powdered snuff that could be inhaled directly. Farmers saw the same benefit in using machines for cutting and processing crops. In 1792, Eli Whitney invented a machine that separated the seeds from the fibers of cotton, and in 1831, Cyrus

McCormick successfully tested a reaping machine that cut wheat and laid it in a straight row for binding into sheaves. Machines replaced hand sewing in the manufacturing of shoes with the first lock-stitch machine invented by Walter Hunt in 1834.

FACTORIES

The next step in America's industrial revolution was the recognition that many individual machines could be combined into a factory for mass production. In 1790, British-born Samuel Slater immigrated to America, bringing with him memorized plans for a textile mill that combined all manufacturing steps within a single building. Upon his arrival, he set to work to create what historians consider America's first factory.

Slater's factory contained machines arranged in a logical layout to streamline the manufacture of textiles. Using water-wheels to drive the machines, wool and cotton were washed, carded, dyed, spun, and finally woven into cloth. The factory not only accelerated the production process, but also decreased the cost of production because operating the machines was less expensive than paying workers. An additional advantage was that machines could run twenty-four hours a day at a constant rate without stopping, except for maintenance and repair. Once other

Pictured here is Eli Whitney's machine for separating cotton fibers from the seeds.

manufacturers saw the benefits of consolidating all of their operations in a single, mechanized factory, all followed Slater's model.

As machinery fed the industrial revolution, iron parts began to replace wooden machinery parts. The iron parts lasted longer than wooden ones, but each was unique and had to be fashioned individually by a skilled craftsperson. Eli Whitney added another important innovation when he recognized the advantage of mass-producing products made with interchangeable parts that could be removed and replaced quickly and inexpensively.

In 1793, Whitney began experimenting with a plan for the mass production of muskets, which until then were individually crafted—often at great expense—by gunsmiths. Whitney recognized that a good musket required dozens of different metal parts. As Whitney thought through the manufacturing process, he recognized that he could mass-produce the parts for the muskets and then the muskets themselves.

FACTORY LABOR

Most of the European immigrants pouring into America during the early nineteenth century either settled in new territories as farmers or provided the labor to run the new factories fueling America's industrial revolution. Those without farming skills tended to settle in large cities, where unskilled workers were needed to operate factory machinery. Immigrants accepted factory work to escape poverty, but the pay was meager. Entire families working in factories was not unusual, regardless of the age of the children. Children regularly grew up in factories and generally worked there all of their lives. Harriet Hanson Robinson, who worked in a garment factory as a young girl and later wrote her autobiography, Lowell Mill Girls, *told of her experiences.*

"The early mill-girls were of different ages. Some were not over ten years old . . . but the majority were between the ages of sixteen and twenty-five. The very young girls were called 'doffers.' They 'doffed,' or took off, the full bobbins from the spinning-frames, and replaced them with empty ones. . . . They were paid two dollars a week. The working hours of all the girls extended from five o'clock in the morning until seven in the evening, with one half-hour each, for breakfast and dinner. Even the doffers were forced to be on duty nearly fourteen hours a day. This was the greatest hardship in the lives of these children."

Robert Fulton's steamboat, the Clermont, *was the first successful steamboat in the United States.*

Not only was Whitney's scheme revolutionary in that it changed manufacturing procedures for a particular product, but also for the first time, machines made the parts that would go into another machine.

The innovations of Whitney and other inventors helped reduce America's dependence on England for manufactured products. These innovations also set the stage for the development of steam-powered machinery that would transport passengers and freight throughout the expanding American frontier.

STEAMBOATS

The first transportation breakthrough in America was the steamboat. Although the invention of the steam engine is attributed to the Scotsman James Watt, the American Robert Fulton adapted this mechanism to power the first successful steamboat in the United States. In 1807, Fulton's first steamboat, the *Clermont*, traveled 145 miles up the Hudson River from New York City to Albany, New York, in thirty hours. This boat could carry more passengers and freight faster and more efficiently than could any form of land travel. By the mid–nineteenth century, hundreds of steamboats, some offering the opulence of floating hotels, plied the major rivers of America as well as along the Atlantic coast. Still, American entrepreneurs recognized that as the westward movement continued and eastern cities grew, the nation would require improved land transportation for both people and products. Once more, steam would power a new means of transport.

FIRST RAILROADS

As cities such as New York, Boston, and Philadelphia grew during the early nineteenth century, more efficient transportation was needed for passengers and freight than canals and steamboats could provide. A rail system linking the major urban centers was the answer. At this time, England led the world in the development of steam-powered locomotives. America imported its first locomotive in 1830 and began an experiment in transportation that would ultimately lead to the fulfillment of the nation's manifest destiny.

The first railroad in America was the Baltimore and Ohio. Initially, this rail line ran only thirteen miles from Baltimore to Ellicott's Mills. But by 1834, the line extended all the way north to Harpers Ferry, West Virginia, and branched over to Washington, D.C. Within fifteen years, New York, Boston, and Chicago also became railroading centers. As railroads extended their reach, the benefits over other modes of travel in speed, reliability, and cost became evident.

The 190-mile trip from New York to Boston, formerly at least a seven-day trip, now could be made by train in a single day. Trains, unlike boats and horses, could travel through the night with little additional risk and could travel nearly as fast in the rain as they could in dry weather.

England was the world leader in developing steam-powered locomotives like the one illustrated here.

Steam-powered trains were a far more reliable means of transportation than horses or steamboats.

Travelers as well as those who shipped goods preferred the reliability of the trains. Reliability meant that perishable food could be transported safely and manufacturers could meet delivery deadlines. Although trains had occasional problems with derailments and breakdowns, they could nonetheless be relied upon far more than horses that traveled muddy roads and needed to be rested frequently or steamboats that were subject to collisions and boiler explosions. To underscore their reliability to the public, the railroads posted arrival and depar-

ture schedules that were accurate to the minute.

With their reliability established, the railroads expanded rapidly. One great advantage of the railroad was its ability to carry larger numbers of passengers and more freight for less money per pound than wagons or boats could, so the cost of passenger travel and freight shipping declined as the nation's railroads grew. Moreover, while boats of any size were limited to major rivers, a train could go anywhere rails could be laid. Shipping costs then dropped as cities located far from water were linked by rail. Since lower freight rates meant lower costs of goods to consumers, gradually the entire nation's well-being came to be linked to the growing rail network.

American inventors, seeing the need for improvements in railroads, set about refining the technology the English had provided. Robert L. Stevens, for example, recognized in 1830 that the English rails, which were made of wood capped with wrought iron, had two flaws. Wood rails lacked the strength to support heavy trains in the first place, and eventually the wood developed dry rot and crumbled. The wrought iron caps similarly lacked the strength to support heavy loads for long periods of time. Cracks and internal flaws caused wrought iron to collapse under the weight of locomotives. To remedy both of these problems, Stevens recommended and developed solid iron rails, which were capable of supporting more weight than wrought iron. Stevens also designed a rail that was broader at the base than at the top, which provided a flange for securing it to the ties. Stevens's design was so successful that it remained in use from then on.

Stevens also recognized that a better fastener was needed to secure the rails to the ties. He invented a hook-headed iron spike that was hammered into the wood ties. The hooked head of the spike had a slight protrusion on one side that secured it to the rail's flange. This hook design prevented the spike from vibrating loose from the rail.

Improvements in locomotives were also needed. English locomotives were small and unsafe. Sparks from engines commonly set fire to passengers' clothing, and cars sometimes detached from the engine on severe inclines, causing the cars to derail and plummet to the bottom. To the primitive, small, steam-powered locomotives were added innovations such as a reverse gear, springs, brakes, and more powerful steam engines capable of pulling more weight. By 1850, steam-powered locomotives weighed forty tons and burned either wood or coal. Passenger and freight cars also improved in quality and safety as their use increased.

Most important, America's industrial capacity had increased to the point where locomotives, cars, rails, and assorted hardware could be manufactured in quantities adequate to connect all of America's eastern commercial centers. Now, those who dreamed of connecting the two coasts saw that technology had brought their vision within reach.

Chapter

3 Linking East and West

If America's manifest destiny was to be fulfilled, the vast open spaces between the West Coast and the Missouri River had to be bridged. Few, if any, Americans thought of the plains, deserts, and mountains as anything but barriers to reaching the West Coast. Three commonly used phrases expressed this idea: the Great American Desert, the Great Void, and the Great Plains all referred to the two thousand miles that stretched between the Missouri River and the Pacific Ocean.

Henry Poor, a railroad engineer and writer who had visited the Great Void, wrote in an 1854 railroad magazine of traveling

> through an uninhabited, and, for the greater part, we may say an uninhabitable country, nearly destitute of wood, extensive districts of it destitute of water; over mountain ranges whose summits are white with eternal snows; over deserts parched under an unclouded sky, and over yawning chasms which the process of disintegration since the volcanic fires were put out, has not yet filled up.[10]

Those who actually crossed the Great Void had excellent reasons to believe a better link between the East and West Coasts was needed. Many pioneers lost family members on the brutal ascents of the two main mountain ranges that stood in their paths, the Rockies and the Sierra Nevada. Snowdrifts could be one hundred feet deep, and avalanches could bury wagon trains unlucky enough to be caught in the mountains during winter.

If mountain snows and desert heat were barriers separating the East from the West, the Indians who inhabited this great piece of the American landscape represented another formidable obstacle. Native Americans viewed the slow migration of white settlers across their land as a threat to their way of life. Consequently, Indians occasionally attacked wagon trains, stealing livestock and killing entire families at the same time.

THE DREAM

Given the obstacles that lay between the Missouri River and California, many people believed that the building of a transcontinental railroad was necessary to fulfill

America's manifest destiny. Others simply saw the railroads as something that should be built just because the technology was available to do so.

In 1858, Henry Poor, editor of *Poor's Manual of Railroads of the United States*, wrote:

> In a railroad to the Pacific we have a great national work, transcending in its magnitude, and in its results, anything yet attempted by man. By its execution, we are to accomplish our appropriate mission, and a greater one than any yet fulfilled by any nation.[11]

By 1860, thousands of miles of railroads linked most of the major cities in the eastern third of the country. Rails all the way across the continent were no longer a matter for the distant future, some believed; they now needed only the production of

Crossing the Rocky Mountains was very dangerous. Brutal winter conditions caused many settlers traveling by wagon trains to lose their lives.

THE DONNER PARTY

One of the primary motivations for building the transcontinental railroad was to provide safe and fast transportation between California and the eastern states. One widely publicized tragedy that underscored the need for the railroad occurred in February 1847 when ninety immigrants heading west to California from Springfield, Illinois, began crossing the Sierra Nevada in the early winter. Lost and trapped in freezing storms, half of the group led by George Donner died. Following a rescue attempt, survivors told of the horrors of being trapped and their desperate acts of cannibalism to stay alive. This eyewitness account, cited in David Colbert's book Eyewitness to the American West, *is taken from the diary of Lewis Keseberg, one member of the group.*

"A heavy storm came up in a few days after the last relief party left. When provisions gave out, I remained four days before I could taste human flesh. There was no other resort—it was that or death. My wife and child had gone on with the first relief party. I knew not whether they were living or dead. For their sakes I must live, if not for my own.

The flesh of starved beings contains little nutrient. It's like feeding straw to horses. I cannot describe the unutterable repugnance with which I tasted the first mouthful of flesh. There is an instinct in our nature that revolts at the thought of touching, much less eating, a corpse. It makes my blood curdle to think of it! Five of my companions had died in my cabin, and their stark and ghastly bodies lay there day and night, seemingly gazing at me with their glazed and staring eyes. I was too weak to move them had I tried.

At midnight, one cold, bitter night, Mrs. George Donner came to my door. She was going alone across the mountain. She was going to start without food or guide. She kept saying, 'My children, I must see my children.' She said she was very hungry, but refused the only food I could offer. She had never eaten the loathsome flesh. She finally lay down, and I spread a feather-bed and some blankets over her. In morning she was dead."

enough iron rails and the hiring of enough workers to spike them into place.

Accompanying America's industrial push forward was the growth in the nation's population. In 1830, the population of the United States was about thirteen million; twenty years later it had reached twenty-three million, and by 1860, thirty-one million. Much of this growth was attributable to European immigrants who came to America hoping to claim land for themselves. A railroad that could move

America's burgeoning population west began to seem a necessity.

Eventually Congress recognized the need for a rail link to California. In 1853, it authorized Secretary of War Jefferson Davis to dispatch survey parties from the Army Corps of Engineers to investigate five possible routes between the Missouri River and the Pacific Ocean. This congressional commitment was vital if a transcontinental railroad was to be built. The money such a venture required was more than could be raised privately. Moreover, the railroad would have to be built on immense tracts of federal land, and only Congress could authorize such a use of the government's property.

U.S. secretary of war Jefferson Davis orchestrated the investigation of possible routes for building the railroad.

Not everyone in Congress favored the project, however. Some members of Congress, for example, saw no advantage to linking East and West. For example, in 1845, Daniel Webster, who opposed the development of the West, asked his colleagues in the U.S. Senate

> What do we want with . . . this region of savages and wild beasts, of deserts of shifting sands and whirlwinds of dust, of cactus and prairie dogs? To what use could we ever put those endless mountain ranges, impenetrable and covered to their bases with eternal snow? What could we do with the western coast line three thousand miles away, rockbound, cheerless, and uninviting?[12]

Opponents in Congress found allies among citizens who saw in railroads an untested technology that somehow conflicted with God's will. In a letter to the editor of the Indiana newspaper, the *Vincennes Western Sun*, one reader wrote:

> Upon the whole, sirs, this railroad is a pestilential, topsyturvy, harumscarum, whirligig scheme. Give me the old, solemn, straightforward regular Dutch canal . . . it is more primitive and scriptural [in keeping with the Bible] and suits a moral and religious people better. . . . [The railroad] will upset all the gravity of the nation.[13]

Other, more practical, individuals simply feared losing money to the railroads. For example, even before Congress officially backed the transcontinental railroad, owners of steamboats plying the

THE PONY EXPRESS

Prior to the railroads, many companies competed for lucrative mail delivery contracts with the U.S. government. The fastest and most reliable mail delivery service between St. Joseph, Missouri, and Sacramento, California, was the Pony Express, which was owned and operated by the Central Overland California and Pikes Peak Express Company. Although its ability to deliver mail is legendary, it remained in business only a year because it proved to be too expensive. Following its demise in 1861, stagecoaches carried the mail until the transcontinental railroad was completed.

A series of horseback riders carried the mail by relay over the two-thousand-mile route between Missouri and California. Each rider rode about ninety miles and received a fresh horse at relay stations about every fifteen miles along the route. The riders worked day and night and averaged ten miles an hour. When the weather was favorable, two runs in each direction were made each week; during the winter runs were made once a week.

Riders were paid extremely well, about one hundred dollars a month, which was equivalent to what successful bankers were paid. The mail they carried, however, cost senders about ten dollars per ounce, which was half the cost of one ounce of gold. The ride through Indian Territory was risky, and advertisements for riders stressed the need for small, thin riders willing to risk death. No deaths to riders ever occurred. The record for mail delivery over the two-thousand-mile route was seven days and seventeen hours, but the average was eight and one-half days.

Missouri River became alarmed about talk of a railroad bridge spanning the river at St. Louis. For them, the railroads represented an unwelcome challenge to their monopoly on moving passengers and freight. The steamboat operators argued that railroad bridges would be an obstruction to river navigation and thus a danger to their steamships. Such complaints would not be sufficient reasons to stop a transcontinental railroad, so the steamboat owners looked for support within the federal government.

In spite of help from Secretary of War Jefferson Davis, who opposed the bridge at St. Louis, after a brief legal battle, the steamboat owners lost. Courts ruled that the construction of the bridge could continue and in April 1856, the 1,535-foot bridge was completed. As one last gesture of opposition, on May 6, a small steamboat rammed one of the piers supporting the bridge, setting the boat on fire. The owners of the boat sued the railroad for damages. Many historians, however, believe the collision was no accident, but was planned to publicize the hazards the bridge posed and to therefore stop the northern route. In the end, the jury was split, and although neither side was awarded the victory, the bridge remained in use.

CHOOSING THE ROUTE WEST

One reason that Congress could not agree on a route was that members realized that whatever city was selected as the railroad's eastern starting point would gain a significant economic and political advantage. Congressmen also bickered over whether the route would be through southern or northern states. According to the Army Corps of Engineers survey parties' reports, all routes were practical, but the southernmost route would be the cheapest because it avoided crossing the highest mountain ranges.

Congressmen from the northern states, however, found a southern route inconceivable. Most of America's manufacturing was in the North, they argued, and needed the fast and cheap transportation a transcontinental railroad could offer. Southerners, although they favored the building of a transcontinental railroad, adamantly opposed a northern route that would run through St. Louis. These politicians wanted a rail line to originate in a major southern city, such as Atlanta or New Orleans, and follow a route through Texas and eventually end in southern California.

Following his review of the reports of the five survey parties, Secretary Davis chose a southern route that started in New Orleans and ended in Los Angeles. His decision came as no surprise, but congressmen from northern states blocked a final decision on the route. Further discussion was curtailed by the outbreak of the Civil War in 1861; if a transcontinental railroad was to be built, it would follow a northern route.

THEODORE JUDAH: A PATRIOTIC VISION

Even as Congress was debating the merits of a northern or southern transcontinental railroad, one visionary had been hard at work building support for a rail line that would begin in Omaha, Nebraska, and end in Sacramento, California. Theodore Judah had designed California's first railroad, which served the gold mining country around Sacramento. Energized by this success with the Sacramento Railroad, Judah dreamed not only of expanding that line but also of linking it with others to provide uninterrupted service between the East Coast and California.

In a pamphlet he wrote in 1857 to promote the Sacramento Railroad, Judah expressed his view of the role a transcontinental railroad could play in fulfilling America's manifest destiny:

And be it remembered that it is not the through lines to California alone upon which the road [the transcontinental railroad] is to rely for through travel. There is Utah, Oregon, Washington, the Russian possessions [Alaska], the Sandwich Islands [Hawaii], China and the Far East Indies—all of which are brought, more or less, within the influence of this road.[14]

Beginning in 1857, Judah made repeated visits to politicians in Washington, D.C., to promote his vision of the railroad. In 1861, he even had discussions with the new president, Abraham Lincoln. Judah's honesty and engineering experience, in addition to his visionary manner, impressed both the president and congressional leaders.

As a result of Judah's persistence, Lincoln's advisers quietly told Judah to get to work organizing a railroad and to be prepared to start work as soon as the president authorized the project. Although there was no guarantee that Lincoln would do so, Judah nonetheless, confidently returned to California to start lining up investors in his dream.

THE BIG FOUR OF THE CENTRAL PACIFIC

In the spring of 1861, while leaders in Washington were debating the details of the transcontinental railroad, Judah traveled to San Francisco in hopes of finding investors for the project. Potential investors, however, nervous about such an unusual undertaking at a time when the nation was at war, brushed off his requests for support; frustrated, Judah returned to Sacramento. There, he chanced to meet four Sacramento merchants who were willing to listen to what he had to say. These men liked what Judah said about the prospects for railroading in California, but most of all they liked the amount of money that they thought could be made from building a transcontinental railroad.

The four men—Mark Hopkins, Charles Crocker, Collis Huntington, and Leland Stanford—had several characteristics in common that made them good candidates as partners with Judah. Ironically, none of

President Abraham Lincoln supported the idea for constructing a railroad to link the east and west.

THE BIG FOUR OF THE CENTRAL PACIFIC

Although the men who were known later as the "Big Four" had no experience running a railroad, all were entrepreneurs willing to take a chance investing in Theodore Judah's idea of building a railroad across the Sierra Nevada. Each of these four men had an interesting background before coming to California.

Mark Hopkins was born in New York State in 1813 and had worked there as a bookkeeper. When gold was discovered in California, he and twenty-five other men formed a company to buy mining equipment and then resell it at a great profit. In 1849 he sailed around Cape Horn to California, where his company collapsed. Frustrated, he went to Sacramento and opened his own hardware store.

By chance, Hopkins's store was next door to a general store owned by Collis Huntington, who had come to California from Connecticut. Huntington never finished school but had an extraordinary ability to memorize numbers. After several years of wandering from job to job, Huntington rushed to California when he heard stories of the gold fields. His motive was not, however, to mine gold but rather to sell goods to the miners. He sold everything from soap to whiskey.

The third man of the Big Four at the meeting was Charles Crocker. Born in New York in 1822, he was physically the biggest of the men, which suited him later when confronting problems with the work crews. Crocker began his career selling apples and oranges. Working sixteen-hour days for thirty cents a day, he caught the gold fever and headed overland for California. Crocker's gruff personality got him to California: After other travelers tried to steal from him, he threatened them at gunpoint. Arriving in Sacramento, he, too, opened a dry goods store.

The last of the four, Leland Stanford, was born in 1824 in New York. His background and experiences were very different from the others. Stanford had been educated as an attorney, and upon his arrival in California, he made a great deal of money mining gold, which he then used to open a grocery store in Sacramento. With his business experience, background in law, and a sizable fortune, he began to dabble in local politics. His political career took off in 1862 when he became governor of California.

the four had any experience in railroading. An important characteristic that each man shared was a willingness to work hard. Also, though, all four had moved to California in hopes of making money. Their dreams of riches were not linked to gold mining but rather to supplying the gold miners with all of their tools, materials, and food.

When Judah completed his presentation to these four men, explaining his proposed route through the Sierra Nevada, he asked for a financial commitment from each man. As businessmen, each saw the potential for a rail line joining California with the rest of the nation. A partnership among the five was struck, creating the Central Pacific Railroad.

In October, Judah headed back to Washington, D.C., to convince congressional leaders to back his proposed route over the Sierra Nevada. He also told Congress that he had lined up the financing needed to get started. Judah was certain that his dream was close to becoming a reality.

THE RAILROAD ACT OF 1862

Events were working in Judah's favor. In the midst of the Civil War, President Lincoln saw the transcontinental railroad as both a commercial as well as a military necessity. With Lincoln's backing, in 1862 Congress passed the Railroad Act, authorizing two companies—the Central Pacific and the Union Pacific—to begin the task of building the transcontinental railroad.

In the end, military and economic considerations, not geographical ones, determined that the eastern terminus would be on the east bank of the Missouri River, at Council Bluffs, Iowa, and the western terminus would be in Sacramento, California, as proposed by Judah. Lincoln understood that moving troops and their supplies was vital to the North's efforts in the Civil War; the economic consideration was that the most direct route between American industry east of the Missouri River and western markets would run through Iowa and Nebraska. Secondarily, some of the congressional leaders who owned property in Council Bluffs and in Sacramento stood to make millions of dollars if the railroad ran between these two cities.

The Railroad Act also specified that the Union Pacific would start construction in Council Bluffs and that the Central Pacific would start in Sacramento. Where the two lines would meet was not specified. The two companies were simply expected to build as quickly as possible until their tracks met.

The Railroad Act also dealt with questions investors raised regarding the ownership of the land on which the track would be laid. Of special interest was how Native American lands were to be treated. The Union Pacific in particular would be crossing territory the federal government had set aside for the Indians. The Railroad Act provided that the government "shall extinguish as rapidly as may be the Indian titles to all lands falling under the operation of this act."[15] In other words, the U.S. government was prepared to revoke rights of ownership to this land without offering the Indians any money in return.

HOMESTEAD ACT OF 1862

President Lincoln saw the need to populate parts of the Midwest as quickly as possible. To encourage families to move east, he authorized Congress to pass the Railroad Act of 1862 and the Homestead Act of 1862. The Homestead Act provided 160 acres to any American citizen who was either the head of a family, twenty-one years old, or a military veteran who had served at least fourteen days.

The act specified that the available land was in the public domain or federally owned land. This vaguely worded description included land in all states except the original thirteen and Maine, Vermont, West Virginia, Kentucky, Tennessee, and Texas. To acquire title to the land, the homesteader had to live on the homestead and farm it for five years. The amount of land made available at no cost to the claimants was 270 million acres—the U.S. government's greatest act of generosity.

The act also specified a few interesting details. Homesteaders who wished to purchase the land rather than work it for the required five years could do so at a cost of $1.25 per acre. The act also specified that creditors could not claim any of the homestead land to remedy debt. Although the homesteaders could farm the land, the U.S. government retained rights to any minerals found under or on the land.

Naturally, another major concern for the investors was how the government would pay for the building of the railroad. Under the law passed by Congress, the U.S. government loaned money to the Union Pacific and the Central Pacific in the form of treasury bonds, which the companies could turn around and sell to the public. How much those bonds would be worth was calculated by the miles of track laid and the type of terrain. Over flatlands the amount was $16,000 per mile; for more difficult terrain the figure doubled to $32,000, and for the most difficult terrain—mountains—the amount rose to $48,000. In addition to these loans, the railroads were given sixty-four hundred acres—ten square miles of federal land for each mile of track laid. Once the government handed the land over to the railroads, they were free to sell it or develop it as they wished.

The railroad owners knew in advance that the value of this acreage would vary depending upon the quality of the land as well as its location. Acreage in the desolate tracts in the remote desert regions of Wyoming, Utah, and Nevada would fetch a low price, while others, rich in mineral deposits or suitable for farming, would bring in considerably more. The railroads' investors also reasoned that acreage close to the tracks would have greater value because of access to the rail line itself. Such locations would naturally be desirable for new towns, further increasing the value of the land.

Even more contentious than financial matters were design specifications. The most hotly contested standard was the track gauge—that is, the distance between the two rails. In the East, rail lines tended to use a gauge of 4 feet, 8½ inches, while lines in California used a gauge of 5 feet. Since the Union Pacific's tracks would

connect with eastern lines, that company favored the narrow gauge, while the Central Pacific favored the wider gauge. In the end, Congress passed a bill setting the gauge at 4 feet, 8½ inches. For the first time in the history of American railroading, trains built to this standard would be able to go anywhere this gauge was used.

In addition to the gauge, the Railroad Act specified that no incline could exceed 116 feet to the linear mile of track and no curve could be tighter than ten degrees. The act also specified types and weights of materials, and most important, stated that all iron rails must be manufactured in the United States. This last stipulation

The Railroad Act of 1862 specified that all iron rails must be manufactured in the United States.

would promote American industry and insure that money spent on the rails would remain in the United States.

The Union Pacific

Of the two companies sharing the building of the transcontinental railroad, the Union Pacific had more of a problem getting under way. One reason was that the company did not have a visionary promoter of the caliber of Theodore Judah. Furthermore, with 163 members on its board of directors, decision making for the Union Pacific was an unwieldy process. Moreover, apathy among board members was a problem. For their first meeting in 1862, only 67 board members even bothered to show up.

The focus of this first meeting was on raising the capital needed for starting construction. Money would eventually come from the federal government, but only after track had been laid. Various money-raising schemes were discussed, including selling bonds, lobbying Congress to get more backing from the government, and selling stock in the new company. Vice President Thomas C. Durant, who had helped in the building of several other railroads, already had been selected to take charge of finances. Durant set about selling stock in the company to raise the needed funds.

Still to be decided was who should serve as chief engineer for the Union Pacific. Just as Theodore Judah was doing for the Central Pacific, the chief engineer would decide the exact route, organize the workers

Vice President Thomas C. Durant was in charge of raising funds to support the construction of the railroad.

into crews with specific responsibilities, and handle all logistical requirements for delivery of construction material. Durant had in mind the man who was currently in charge of all railroads operated by the Union army, General Grenville Dodge. Durant asked Dodge to quit the army to help the Union Pacific start construction, but he refused. Durant's second choice was Peter Dey, who had a reputation as an experienced and reliable railroad engineer. Dodge called Dey "the most eminent engineer of the country, [a man] of great ability, [known for] his uprightness, and the square deal he gave everyone."[16]

The difficulty of finding a chief engineer was only a small part of a much larger personnel problem. The thousands of men needed to swing sledgehammers, lift rails in place, and perform hundreds of other backbreaking jobs were fighting in the Civil War. Given the severe labor shortage, Durant reported to the other members of the Union Pacific's board of directors that construction of the railroad could not possibly start on time.

THE RAILROAD ACT OF 1864

Meanwhile, both the Central Pacific and the Union Pacific believed that the task they had set for themselves could not be completed without additional money. In 1864, Thomas Durant, representing the Union Pacific, and Collis Huntington, representing the Central Pacific, went to Congress to ask for more aid from the federal government. The two men arrived in Washington with suitcases full of cash and railroad stock certificates, to be used to influence key members of Congress and secure the needed votes. What Durant and Huntington sought, and finally got, was a doubling of the land grants from the original 6,400 acres per mile of track to 12,800 acres, as well as rights to all iron and coal located under that land. The companies also received the right to sell their own bonds to the public in addition to the U.S. Treasury bonds. With this extra help, both companies now had the financial muscle needed to complete the enormous project to which they had committed themselves.

4 The Central Pacific: East Across the Sierra Nevada

Theodore Judah knew that the route he had chosen for the Central Pacific would be tough right from the start. From Sacramento, the railroad would climb almost immediately into the most ferocious mountain terrain in the country. Judah estimated that the first hundred miles of track would take longer to build than all the rest, but working in the mountains had some advantages. Water would be plentiful, as would the much-needed timber for the bridges and railroad ties. As for manpower, Judah began running advertisements in local newspapers, hoping to hire miners who had given up on their attempts to find gold.

HEADING OUT AND UP

The groundbreaking ceremony for the Central Pacific took place amid long-winded speeches by leading Sacramento residents like Collis Huntington on January 8, 1863. Not everyone was in an optimistic mood, however. Huntington, for one, foresaw the difficulties that lay ahead:

If you want to jubilate over driving the first spike, go ahead and do it. I don't. Those mountains over there look ugly. We may fail, and if we do, I want to have as few people know it as we can. . . . Anybody can drive the first spike, but there are many months of labor and unrest between the first and last spike.[17]

But it was not until October 26 of that year that the first spike was driven for the Central Pacific. Two weeks after the first spike had been driven, the first locomotive arrived in California at a cost of $13,688. Weighing forty-six tons when fully loaded with water and coal, it stood ten feet tall and fifty feet long. Named Governor Stanford after the railroad's partner, who had by now been elected as his state's leader, the gold lettering "C.P.R.R." proudly proclaimed its ownership.

Simply getting the Governor Stanford to Sacramento had been an enormous task. All railroad equipment made of iron or steel was produced on the East Coast and shipped on long voyages around the tip of South America. For the duration of the project, all materials the Central Pacific used would cost more than those the Union Pacific used and would arrive in a somewhat haphazard manner.

As rail beds were cleared and logs were cut for trestles across rivers, Judah pushed ahead, surveying the precise route for the railroad. Working outdoors solving engineering problems was where Judah was happiest. Unfortunately, as one of the five partners in the Central Pacific, he had to struggle with business concerns that only distantly related to the actual building of the railroad. He also had to struggle with his partners, Stanford, Crocker, Huntington, and Hopkins.

SQUEEZING OUT JUDAH

Judah's partners, known to historians as the Big Four, focused exclusively on the money to be made from building the railroad, not its later operation. Their objective, therefore, was to build the railroad as cheaply as possible. Judah's position, on the other hand, was that his task was to build the best-engineered railroad possible. This difference in objective placed a strain on the relationship between Judah and his partners from the start.

The Governor Stanford was the first locomotive to arrive in California.

The conflict over costs flared when the Big Four learned that building the railroad through a mountain pass other than the one chosen by Judah could save the company hundreds of thousands of dollars in construction costs. Judah knew that the pass his partners favored was not suitable for a railroad, because the ground was unstable and would wash away in heavy rains. He therefore refused to permit a change of plans. The Big Four also bickered with Judah endlessly about the safety of the construction workers, the amount of lumber needed to build safe bridges, and the amount of gravel needed to hold the rails in place around bends in the road. In all cases, Judah advocated for the soundest construction standards, which always translated into the most expensive construction. Opposed every step of the way by the Big Four, and realizing that they were interested only in short-term profits, Judah grew frustrated. He wrote to his wife, Anna:

> I cannot make these men appreciate the "Elephant" they have on their shoulders, they won't do what I want and must do. We shall just as sure have troubles in Congress as the sun rises in the east if they go on in this way. Something must be done. I have brought them a franchise and laid it at their door . . . and they would beggar [bankrupt] it.[18]

As Judah's frustration with his partners increased, he offered to buy them out. The Big Four refused to discuss his offer, knowing that they stood to make enormous profits from the enterprise. Judah, convinced that he was right, persisted in his buyout effort, even going so far as to enlist the aid of a famous multimillionaire, Cornelius Vanderbilt. Judah decided to travel to Vanderbilt's home in New York to discuss with him the possibility of offering the Big Four enough money to convince them to sell. That meeting never took place, however. While crossing the Isthmus of Panama, Judah became ill with yellow fever and died in New York on November 2, 1863. His plan of eliminating the Big Four from the Central Pacific died with him.

Even before Judah died, however, his partners were busy seeing to it that they, not Judah, would make the greatest profit from the railroad. As soon as Judah departed for New York, the Big Four quickly began making deals among themselves that excluded Judah. Since they knew the railroad's route based on Judah's surveying, they began buying acreage along the route that the railroad would follow, offering the smallest amounts possible to further increase their profits. The Big Four also held private meetings in Judah's absence to overrule many of his engineering decisions that they believed to be too costly.

THE CHINESE

To observers, it must have seemed that the Central Pacific had virtually an impossible task cut out for it. The path through the Sierra Nevada was recognized by both railroad companies as the toughest geographical challenge. The

Workers uncover a snowed-in length of track. Severe winter conditions made construction of the railroad very difficult.

Sierra Nevada are virtually solid granite cut by deep ravines through which run torrents of water. Tunneling through that granite and building trestles across icy rivers were made all the more difficult by severe winters lasting six months.

Aside from the rigors of the terrain, the Central Pacific faced severe manpower shortages, just as the Union Pacific did. Most men available to work on the Central Pacific were reluctant to leave the gold fields where they hoped to strike it rich. Although few were successful, it was hard to find men willing to perform the backbreaking work of swinging twelve-pound sledgehammers in the Sierra Nevada for two dollars a day. Charles Crocker even advertised in New York and Boston newspapers, hoping to recruit Irish immigrants looking for work. At considerable expense, Crocker shipped two thousand men who had agreed to work on the railroad to San Francisco. As soon as they arrived in California, however, nineteen hundred of his recruits fled to the gold fields. In desperation, Crocker then tried getting government permission to hire Confederate prisoners of war, but the War Department rejected his request. He later tried hiring newly emancipated slaves, but had no more success than he had with the Irish in convincing them to work on the railroad.

The labor shortage became more acute as the railroad slowly moved higher into the mountains. The lead construction foreman, Jim Strobridge, finally told Crocker that they could never achieve their objective without more workers. Crocker's reply was to suggest trying a previously untapped source of labor, the Chinese.

At this time, an estimated sixty thousand Chinese, nearly all men, were living in California. The Chinese, like men from virtually every country in the world, had come to California in search of gold. And like their fellow prospectors, most Chinese had found not instant riches but only frustration and poverty. Crocker reasoned that if nobody else would agree to help build the railroad, perhaps the Chinese might do so.

Strobridge was convinced that the Chinese, because they tended to be of shorter stature than whites, lacked the strength and stamina to perform the physically demanding tasks involved in building the railroad. Crocker, however, reminded him that the Chinese, after all, had built the Great Wall of China. Reluctantly, Strobridge agreed to give a few Chinese a try. Part of what motivated Strobridge was that the price of labor would be right. Frederick F. Low, a former governor of California and minister to China, revealed to the San Francisco newspaper, the *Daily Alta Californian*, that,

> I was one of the commissioners when the Pacific Railroad was in the course of construction on this [west] side of the Sierra Mountain Range. . . . They paid the Chinese $31 a month, and they boarded [fed] themselves. To the white laborers they professed to pay, and did pay, $45 a month and board, which amounted, they considered, to two dollars a day.[19]

Although the Chinese were paid considerably less than their white coworkers, these wages were nonetheless, twice what they could make in San Francisco. Strobridge organized a couple of hundred Chinese into crews of ten to twenty men and placed each group under the direction of a white foreman.

After a month, Strobridge realized that he had underestimated his new workers. Beginning with lighter tasks such as fixing meals and caring for the horses, they were quickly promoted to the most difficult jobs, such as drilling and dynamiting. Years

Chinese immigrants were hired to work on the railroad.

later, in 1876, Crocker was called to testify before a joint congressional committee investigating the use of Chinese labor for the building of the transcontinental railroad. During his testimony, Crocker summarized the Central Pacific's experience with the Chinese:

We commenced with white labor . . . [but] could not get sufficient labor to progress with the road [rails] as fast as was necessary, and felt driven to the experiment of trying Chinese labor. . . . I had charge of the construction, and Mr. Strobridge was under

STROBRIDGE

Jim Strobridge was a relentless foreman who tyrannically kept the Central Pacific moving east. Just over six feet tall, the Irishman towered above nearly everyone, especially the Chinese, whose height rarely exceeded five feet. Strobridge's face had the look of a man who had been in many a fistfight, and few dared to challenge him. Part of his ability to intimidate obstinate workers stemmed from the patch he wore over one eye that he lost as a result of a blasting accident. Strobridge had entered a tunnel after a blast, unaware that one of the long fuses leading to a charge was still burning. When the powder blew, a piece of granite embedded in his eye. Workers who feared him claimed that he pulled the granite chip from his eye and kept directing operations. This incident earned him a nickname among the Chinese: "One-eyed Boss Man."

Strobridge's hard work and willingness to suffer through the severe winters side by side with the crews earned him a reputation as a fair man. His willingness to confront groups of angry men with an ax handle earned him the reputation as a tough man willing to fight to get his way. Although he opposed the hiring of Chinese at the start of the push up the Sierra Nevada, he was quick to recognize that they were the equal of any group. Strobridge gradually put them on every type of task except managing other crews.

me as superintendent. He thought that the Chinese would not answer [to offers of employment] considering what they eat, and other things, and from what he had seen of them; he did not think they were fit laborers; he did not think they would build a railroad. . . . [We] tried them on the light work, thinking they would not do for heavy work. Gradually we found that they did well there, and as our forces spread out and we occupied more ground, and felt more in a hurry, we put them into the softer cuts, and finally into the rock cuts. Where ever we put them we found them good, and they worked themselves into our favor to such an extent that if we found we were in a hurry for a job, it was better to put on Chinese at once.[20]

CONQUERING THE SIERRA NEVADA

The construction crews made good progress at first. By June 1864, the Central

Pacific had completed 42 miles of track from Sacramento through the Sierra Nevada foothills to Clipper Gap, a small lumber settlement. Here the crews would begin the arduous assault of the Sierra Nevada themselves, as the route Judah had laid out wound up mountain passes and across ravines. Workers built several trestles 400 to 500 feet long, standing as high as 90 feet above the coursing rivers below. By late September, the rails stretched 54 miles from Sacramento and had reached an elevation of 2,200 feet. From here to the summit, as surveyed by Judah, the route would climb almost another 5,000 feet over a 50-mile distance. The Railroad Act of 1862 specified that inclines could not exceed 116 feet per mile. The push to the summit would test this limit.

Railroad trestles were built to cross rivers and ravines. They were often 400 to 500 feet long and stood as high as 90 feet above the ground.

A City on Wheels

Each railroad maintained a train that closely followed the rail crews. The train provided all sorts of specialty cars to meet the needs of the crew. Each of the cars functioned like a small business on wheels, catering to the needs of the workmen. At the peak of rail setting, the Union Pacific supported a work crew of eight thousand. Providing for their needs, especially since they were often more than a hundred miles from a major city, required a city on wheels.

Repairing equipment for thousands of workers was primarily the job of the blacksmiths. Most of the tools on the railroad were made of iron and were in constant need of repair or sharpening after repeated chiseling and drilling through granite. Picks, sledgehammers, and shovels also needed constant repair or modification for special needs.

The carpenters' car, just like the blacksmiths' car, was a place for repairs and construction of unusual implements. Building wood trestles across rivers, repairing broken wood wagon wheel spokes, and replacing wood handles on picks and shovels kept these men busy.

Horses and mules moved men and material forward ahead of the trains. These thousand-pound animals had many special needs. The feed car carried oats and corn in territory where grass was sparse. Sick animals visited the veterinarian, who carried boxes full of remedies as well as basic operating instruments. Hooves, the biggest source of horse ailments, were kept clipped, cleaned, and free of the rot that was common in wet terrain.

Following dinner, many of the crew chose to sleep in large dormitory cars. Photos of these cars show them much larger than any of the other cars. Eighty-five feet long, ten feet high, and ten feet wide, dormitory cars were short on privacy when all 180 bunks were filled, but they kept workers dry.

Trains with large specialty cars followed rail crews in order to provide services to the workers.

On July 5, 1865, the first town in the Sierra Nevada the railroaders reached was Dutch Flats, 65 miles from Sacramento. This 23-mile stretch from Clipper Gap had taken an entire year, and now the work was measured in feet per day. But the worst was yet to come: Avoiding steep grades that would exceed the 116-foot-per-mile incline limit required the digging of tunnels and long, looping roadbeds along the sheer face of the granite mountains. The looping technique was used instead of switchbacks because, as specified in the Railroad Act of 1862, engineers had to avoid curves sharper than ten degrees.

CAPE HORN

Occasionally, the route Judah had chosen seemed to present insurmountable problems. One three-mile stretch, called Cape Horn by the workers, was unsuitable for tunneling because the mountain was so large and the slope was too steep for a straight grade or loops. Instead, workers cut a roadbed that skirted the edge of the mountain. More than a thousand feet below, the American River churned by. The work was exceptionally dangerous because on such steep terrain, men and horses could easily lose their footing, and a fall meant almost certain death.

At this point, Crocker's decision to employ Chinese laborers paid an extra dividend. Hoping to speed up the work, a delegation of Chinese approached Strobridge in the summer of 1865 and proposed a solution to the problem posed by

cutting a rail bed along the steep cliffs. The Chinese said that similar problems in China had been overcome by workers using wicker baskets hung from the cliffs above as work platforms. The idea was to lower workmen down the face of the cliff in the baskets. Strobridge was willing to try anything at this point and ordered reeds to be sent up the mountain. Quickly, the Chinese wove the reeds into baskets and set to work.

Dangling precariously on the mountain face in dozens of baskets, the Chinese would drill holes in the granite, fill them with black powder, light the fuse, and then shout to workers above to pull them clear before the powder exploded. This new procedure speeded up the work, but at a terrible price. Not all baskets were pulled out of harm's way fast enough, and several Chinese workers were blown up as a result.

One reason that progress on Cape Horn was so slow was that roadbeds had to be cut wide enough to accommodate more than just one set of rails. Room was needed for sidings to allow one train to pull over while a second one passed; room for work sheds was also needed. Consequently, dynamiting had to clear as much as a one-hundred-foot-wide roadbed around much of Cape Horn.

The tedious work of chiseling a roadbed out of a steep mountainside, along with tunneling and building trestles in the Sierra Nevada, demanded as many men as the Central Pacific could find. With the exception of the U.S. Army, the Central Pacific's crew of ten thousand men, eight thousand of whom were Chinese, was at

Nitroglycerin was used in blasting but was soon abandoned due to the number of workers that were killed using it.

the time the largest workforce in the North American continent.

TUNNEL NUMBER 6

Creating the long loops of Cape Horn was challenging enough, but on thirteen different occasions, tunnels were required. The longest and most difficult of these was Tunnel Number 6. Located at Donner Summit at an elevation of just over seven thousand feet, it was named Summit Tunnel. Also known to the crews as Tunnel Number 6, this tunnel presented the toughest job of all: blasting through a quarter mile of solid granite.

Time was of the essence to Crocker and his partners, because although crews were being paid by the day, the government was paying the railroads by the mile of completed track. Therefore, to speed progress, Crocker ordered work to begin at both ends of the tunnel simultaneously. Also, as far as Crocker was concerned, working inside of a tunnel meant that day and night were all the same. Consequently, he ordered that blasting continue around the clock in three eight-hour shifts.

The work was arduous and agonizingly slow. To split granite, black powder was poured into holes drilled fifteen to eighteen inches deep. Hand-operated drills took hours to reach the required depths. Sledgehammers and chisels were also used for this process. Both drill bits and chisels dulled within a few minutes, and sharpening them was tedious and time-consuming. Once the required depth was reached, powder was packed into the hole and a fuse attached. The fuse would be lit, someone would yell, "Fire in the hole!" and workers would run for safety. Most of the time, workers would get out of the tunnel in time to avoid the blast—but not always. The Central Pacific did not keep statistics, but estimates of the number of workers killed in such blasts range in the hundreds.

To speed up the blasting process, the Central Pacific experimented with a new, more powerful explosive called nitroglycerin ("nitro"). Although more rock could be loosened with this new liquid explosive, nitro, had the disadvantage of being highly unstable. In warm weather, it could detonate simply by being spilled or shaken. On other occasions, a pocket of nitro would fail to explode until a worker accidentally struck it with his pick. The blast of nitro was so powerful that no identifiable body parts of workmen blown up in accidents like these could be found. After a number of workers were killed this way, the use of nitro was abandoned.

Progress on Tunnel Number 6 averaged between six and twelve inches a day. The amount of black powder used for blasting in this one tunnel averaged five hundred kegs per day—each keg weighing twenty-five pounds. The cost just for blasting powder was a staggering two thousand dollars per day. By the time the Central Pacific had completed all thirteen tunnels, the amount of black powder expended was more than the total amount of powder used for guns and cannons by the combined armies in the Civil War.

THE BLACK GOOSE

Winter hit the Sierra Nevada harder than usual in 1865 and slowed work even more. Snow covered much of the track on the western slope of the Sierra Nevada, preventing supply trains from delivering needed tools, blasting powder, rails, and food. Grading and blasting crews were diverted from their work in order to clear snow, slowing the progress through Donner Summit further still.

Something had to be done to remedy the constant blocking of the tracks during the winter. The snow problem forced engineers to find a way of diverting avalanches off the tracks. Their idea was to cover the most susceptible stretches of track with wood roofs. The roofs were tucked against the mountainside and sloped down toward the cliff side of the tracks so that when an avalanche would roll down the mountain, the tumbling snow would slide across the roof, falling harmlessly into the ravine below.

Sometimes mud became the enemy. Foul weather conditions forced the Central Pacific to move supplies on pack animals, but mud impeded the progress of the sturdy mules. To make matters worse, heavy rains at lower elevations washed tons of mud onto tracks that had been cut through low-lying hills. Still more men were diverted from blasting to clear the mud away and to shore up eroded rail beds.

Because the harsh winter had slowed work so much, ingenuity was required

---

MEALTIME

The tedium of hard, physical labor made meals the high point of the day for the crews. Although the meals could become boring, the railroads tried to serve them hot as often as possible. All three daily meals were large. The railroads tried to meet the diverse needs of the men as best they could.

Most popular for the predominantly Irish crew of the Union Pacific was boiled beef, beans, potatoes, bread, and coffee. To meet the need for beef, the Union Pacific moved a herd of cattle along with the crews. As the Union Pacific railroad moved across the plains, women from small towns along the way saw an opportunity to make money selling fresh baked goods to the crews. Recognizing that homemade goods boosted morale, railroad officials occasionally purchased fresh bread, dough-nuts, pies, and milk.

Rice was the staple for the predominantly Chinese crew of the Central Pacific. They demanded, and received at their own expense, delicacies such as dried and salted fish, large assortments of fruits shipped to them from the California valleys, as well as eggs, tomatoes, pickles, and tea. The tea was carried in cleaned empty powder kegs, which earned the tea its name, "gunpowder tea." On special occasions, the Chinese ate deli-cacies such as abalone, oysters, pork, chicken, and mushrooms.

Both railroads provided dining cars, but the crews preferred to eat their own meals out of doors. If the weather was cold or rainy, however, the crews packed into the dining cars and ate on long tables that could accommodate one hundred men at a time.

Breakfast was eaten after the men had dressed and washed, and was as big a meal as lunch or dinner. The hard, physical work required about six thousand calories a day. Lunch was a one-hour break whenever the foreman called it out—usually at noon, although 1:00 or 1:30 P.M. was not unusual. Dinner followed the end of the workday at sunset and was the most relaxed meal of the day.

to get work back on schedule. To complete Tunnel Number 6 more quickly, Crocker and Strobridge decided to cut a vertical shaft through the center of the mountain to enable workers to dig the tunnel from the middle outward toward both ends. The shaft, eight feet by twelve feet, was cut down to the level of the roadbed seventy-three feet below the mountaintop. As rock was blasted loose, it was then hauled to the surface. This process was agonizingly slow, but once again the builders came up with an ingenious solution. A small locomotive, named the Black Goose, was adapted to hoist debris out of the shaft.

The Black Goose steamed up to the end of the tracks. Workers then dismantled the locomotive and hauled it piece by piece on wagons pulled by oxen up to the summit. At the top of the shaft, workers reassembled the Black Goose and attached ropes to the driving wheels of the locomotive. As the wheels turned, they hoisted debris out of the tunnel. This unusual application of a locomotive hastened the completion of Tunnel Number 6 and helped get the project back on schedule.

THE RACE IS ON

The delays the Central Pacific encountered in the Sierra Nevada were costly not only because of the wages paid to the construction crews. The Railroad Act of 1862 had precisely established the starting point for both railroads but had not specified the meeting point. This omission had made sense at the time because no one knew how fast each company could build the rail line. Still, how much track a company laid directly affected the amount of money it made. So when managers of the Union Pacific learned of the problems the Central Pacific was having blasting through the Sierra Nevada, they decided to take advantage of the situation by sending out surveying parties far beyond where the Union Pacific's track layers were working.

Crocker saw that his company stood to lose millions of dollars in federal money if the Union Pacific managed to lay track in territory that the Central Pacific might otherwise have claimed. Crocker hit on a solution that was sure to foil the Union Pacific's scheme but which risked bankruptcy for the Central Pacific. He brought an entirely new crew of workers to the eastern slope of the Sierra Nevada to push ahead in the Truckee Valley with grading, trestle building, and track laying.

The risk in Crocker's bold move was that the government funds were paid only upon completion of continuous stretches of track. Until the line into the Truckee Valley connected to the track that was inching through the Sierra Nevada, the Central Pacific was not going to receive federal money, nor would it be allowed to sell the land promised in the original legislation. To lower the financial risks, the Central Pacific petitioned Congress to allow them to build ahead of the eastern railhead. On June 19, 1866, the Congress passed an amendment to the original Railroad Act, allowing the Central Pacific to "locate, construct and continue their road east-

In a letter to Collis Huntington (left), Mark Hopkins described the Central Pacific's victory over the Sierra Nevada.

ward, in a continuous, completed line, until they shall meet and connect with the Union Pacific Railroad."[21] This congressional decision was significant to the Central Pacific in a second way: Tracks across the Nevada desert would generate profits faster than profits derived from blasting through the granite of the Sierra Nevada.

And the money, as far as the railroads' investors were concerned, was what this whole effort was about. While Americans were becoming excited about the prospects of the transcontinental railroad linking the two coasts, those investing in the railroads were excited about how much money they could make. In a letter to Collis Huntington, Mark Hopkins wrote, "We're pushing hard. For as we see it . . .

the road will earn us a heap . . . and we can make a pile [of money]."[22]

At the eastern side of the Sierra Nevada, crews anticipating the completion of Tunnel Number 6 also began laying track from the Truckee Valley west to Donner Summit. Building this isolated stretch was particularly arduous. Trains on the western side of the summit hauled thousands of tons of construction supplies as far as the rails could take them. At the end of the rails, workers loaded all materials onto wagons and carted them over the pass and down the eastern slope. The foremen wanted to move forward so quickly that in November 1866, workers near the summit placed two locomotives on wood sleds greased with

THE TEN-MILE DAY

Track-laying competitions had taken place for many months between the crews of the Central Pacific and Union Pacific. Each time the number of miles of track increased until the Union Pacific laid eight miles. In mid-April 1869, the track-laying competition between the two railroads reached its peak when Crocker wagered Durant ten thousand dollars that the Central Pacific could lay a record setting ten miles of track in a single day.

These track-laying competitions delighted financiers who knew that they would make sixteen thousand dollars per level mile in addition to 12,800 acres of land for each mile of track. The crews also appeared to enjoy the competitive spirit in what was in reality a competition between the Chinese and the Irish.

As the sun rose, the race was on. Chinese workers unloaded sixteen carts of rails, spikes, connecting plates, and wood ties in the first eight minutes. Following the distribution of materials, a team of eight rail setters, four to each 560-pound rail, picked up the two rails with their tongs and dropped them in place. Then the spiking crews nailed the rails in place, straightening crews made sure the rails were parallel and exactly 4 feet, 8½ inches apart, and finally crushed gravel was tamped in place. The moment the tamping was done, the next load of material was run down the line and the process repeated itself.

By mid-morning, this assembly line of Central Pacific workers was one thousand men long and was setting rails at a record pace of one mile per hour. In the midst of this army of workers, foremen rode back and forth on horseback shouting encouragement while others carried cups of tea to the Chinese workers. By lunchtime, the crew had laid six miles of track. Confident of success, the crews took a full hour for their meal.

By dinnertime at 7:00 P.M., the crews reached just beyond the ten-mile mark. The crews had set more than 24,000 ties, 3,522 rails, 3,520 fish plates, 55,000 pounds of spikes, and 14,000 pounds of bolts. Each of the eight rail setters had lifted 124 tons of iron while walking hunched over ten miles down the track, and each received a bonus equal to four days' wages. Excluding the one-hour lunch break, the crew raced along at the rate of eighty feet per minute—just under one mile per hour. This record was never beaten.

animal fat on their undersides. With the muscle of hundreds of laborers and dozens of mule teams, the locomotives were pulled over the summit.

With the help of the Black Goose, Tunnel Number 6 was now progressing from both ends and the middle simultaneously. At the end of 1866, twelve of the thirteen tunnels had been finished, and the track led ninety-two miles from Sacramento. Twelve miles still separated the end of the line from Donner Summit. It would not be until August 1867 that the breakthrough of Tunnel Number 6 would happen, and not until December of that year that the track would be laid.

Once the Donner Summit was conquered, the process for the Central Pacific was literally a downhill run east. In a letter to Collis Huntington, Mark Hopkins commented, "Yesterday we all went up to see the first locomotive pass the summit of the Sierra. . . . We are now on the downgrade and we rejoice. . . . [Tunnel Number 6] was a thing never before done."[23] But the cost had been horrendous. The tough miles going over the Sierra Nevada had earned the Central Pacific $48,000 per mile in payments, while the actual cost per mile of construction had been $246,000. Both the owners and the Chinese workers looked forward to easier and more profitable times laying rail on flat land.

RACING ACROSS THE DESERT

Tough as the push through Donner Summit was, the race across the flat Nevada desert posed its own challenges for the Central Pacific. Thirst was a problem for both workers and pack animals, since water was in short supply in this parched wasteland. Besides water, the Central Pacific was short of rails. Because it still took six months to ship construction materials like rails around the tip of South America, crews were limited in how fast they could lay track. Crocker had earlier promised to lay one mile of track a day through Nevada—but that was impossible. To speed delivery of rails, the Central Pacific decided to order them shipped across the Isthmus of Panama. This decision, though, greatly increased the costs. The final cost when the rails shipped this way arrived in San Francisco was $143 a ton. Since each thirty-foot rail weighed 560 pounds, shipping enough rails across Panama to fill the Central Pacific's needs threatened to bankrupt the company. Even so, in July Huntington notified Crocker that he had shipped 60,000 tons to San Francisco with an additional 90,000 tons scheduled by the close of the year. Locomotives presented a similar problem. In 1865, one engine cost $35,350 at the East Coast factory and an additional $8,000 to ship.

In spite of the problems, at the beginning of 1868, both railroads were racing to get as far as possible. Now the project began to resemble a fierce competition. One day after the Union Pacific's management bragged in newspapers that its crew had laid four miles of track in one day, the Central Pacific responded by laying six miles. This in turn drove the Union Pacific to extend the workday to eighteen hours in order to lay eight miles of track a day.

The competition to lay track was intensified by the fact that no meeting point for the two lines had yet been set. Both railroads sent out grading crews many miles ahead of the actual track-laying crews. In their enthusiasm to grab the right to build as many miles of track as possible, the grading crews from the two companies actually began to pass each other, creating a situation in which they were working parallel to each other but in opposite directions. To rectify this situation, a government commission finally designated Promontory Summit, Utah, as the meeting point for the two lines. In April, when each line's rails were about fifteen miles from Promontory Summit, the grading crews stopped their work. They would go no farther.

On April 30, 1869, the Central Pacific reached Promontory Summit, 690 miles from its start in Sacramento. Remarkably, of those miles, the first 119 to the summit of the Sierra Nevada took four and one half years. The remaining 571 miles had taken just over one year to complete.

5 The Union Pacific: West Across the Great Plains

With the end of the Civil War, the Union Pacific had solved its immediate problem of a labor shortage. And given the Central Pacific's difficulties in the Sierra Nevada, it might have appeared that the Union Pacific's task would be easier. The Union Pacific's surveyors chose a route that was flat, straight, and close to water. Still, one problem remained: finding a leader to oversee the construction effort.

Grenville Dodge was chosen to lead the construction of the Union Pacific Railroad.

Peter Dey had resigned as chief engineer. This time, Thomas Durant was able to convince Grenville Dodge to lead the construction of the Union Pacific. Dodge was uniquely qualified for the job. Born in 1831, he had spent all of his life around railroads. President Lincoln had chosen Dodge to oversee the railroad building in the Union for the duration of the war. Moreover, Dodge knew the territory where the Union Pacific would be working. When he was twenty-two years old and working for the small M&M Railroad in Missouri, he had surveyed the Platte River and believed that one day it would be a perfect location for a railroad.

A LATE START

Dodge's first challenge was to make up for the two years that had been lost because of labor shortages. The Railroad Act of 1862 required the Union Pacific to complete their first one hundred miles of track by June 27, 1866, but a lack of workers made that goal seem unattainable. Clearly, an extraordinary organizational effort would have to be put forth if that deadline was to be met.

The first mile of the Union Pacific took eleven days to complete. Workers were later promised bonuses if they could lay down one-and-a-half miles of track per day.

To organize the workforce, Durant hired two brothers, John and Dan Casement, to oversee the track work and the project's finances. John Casement had earned a reputation as a fearless and rugged leader during the Civil War. Casement was willing to drive the men relentlessly to perform whatever work Durant needed. Characteristic of his management style was that he regularly carried a bullwhip and a .44 caliber pistol strapped to his waist.

The Casement brothers quickly hired any able-bodied man tough enough to work twelve-hour days and willing to do so without complaint for one dollar a day plus food. Civil War veterans from the armies of both the North and the South signed up, along with many unemployed Irish immigrants from Boston and New York. By the summer of 1865, John Casement had the crews working at full speed.

Prospects of meeting the late June deadline were still bleak. Durant had promised investors that his crews would lay two miles of track a day, but once work finally commenced, the first mile took eleven days to complete. Still short of workers, he admitted in September 1865 that he would be lucky to complete sixty miles by December. In fact, by December 31 of that year, the Union Pacific had managed to complete only forty miles.

Casement was under tremendous pressure to meet the 100-mile mark by the deadline. He promised his men bonuses if they could lay 1½ miles a day, and later doubled their wages for each day they laid 2 miles of track. Casement's tactics paid off. On June 16, eleven days ahead of schedule, his crews reached the 100-mile mark. By August the "Casement Army," as it was now called, had spiked an astonishing 191 miles of rails. That rate of progress was not to hold, however.

If the Central Pacific had the Sierra Nevada as its greatest challenge, the Union

Pacific had to contend with opposition from the Indians. As the cold winds of autumn began to blow across the Great Plains, many of the Indian tribes watching the rapid advance of the rails began to recognize the threat posed by the "Iron Horse," as they aptly referred to the trains. In an attempt to stop the advance of the railroad, Indians began raids on the surveying and grading crews.

FIRST THE INDIANS

Now Dodge's primary worry changed from hiring enough workers to dealing with the Indians. Attacks against white settlers and railroad surveying crews had been occurring for some time. For example, in 1865, a combined force of Sioux, Cheyenne, and Arapaho Indians raided Julesburg, Colorado, killing fifteen U.S. soldiers. They then burned the entire town and attacked farms along the Platte River. More disturbing to Dodge, the violence was taking place in the area where his

crews would be working. Henry Morton Stanley, a visiting reporter from England, was traveling throughout Nebraska at this time. He reported back to England that within a thirty-one-mile stretch of land surveyed for the Union Pacific, he had encountered "no less than ninety-three graves; twenty-seven of which contained the bodies of settlers killed within the last six weeks. Dead bodies have been seen floating down the Platte [River]."[24]

Events soon proved Dodge's fears to be well founded, and he responded accordingly. Following several Indian attacks against surveying crews, Dodge issued an order calling on his men to aggressively respond to such incidents:

> Place every mounted man in your command on the South Platte route; repair telegraph lines, attack all bodies of hostile Indians large or small; stay with them and pound them until they move north of the Platte [River] or south of the Arkansas [River]. I am coming with two regiments of the

One of the many dangers the work crews faced was being attacked by Native Americans.

cavalry to the Platte line and will open and protect it.[25]

Dodge knew that he had the army's backing for this order. At this point, the highest-ranking generals in the U.S. Army had taken a position against the territorial rights of the Indians on railroad property. General Ulysses Grant had authorized the removal of all trespassers from land that had been granted to the Union Pacific.

So aggressive was Dodge's campaign against the Indians that Durant became worried that Dodge had lost sight of his original objective: to build a railroad. When Durant reminded Dodge that his primary responsibility was as chief engineer to the Union Pacific, Dodge responded that until the Indians were removed, there would be no railroad across the Great Plains.

Surveyors threatened to quit unless the railroad brought soldiers to protect them. The directors of the Union Pacific, however, viewed the sporadic Indian attacks as lacking any long-term consequence. They ordered Dodge and the Casement brothers to push on with the surveys.

The directors were correct in seeing the attacks as isolated incidents, but they erred in believing that the consequences were minor. Until the surveyors could stake the route farther west, no rails could be laid, and only after the rails had been laid could the Union Pacific get the money that the government promised. Yet, Dodge believed the Indians could not possibly win this fight and would be forced to eventually withdraw from the path of the railroad. In this regard, British

observer Henry Stanley agreed. After attending a meeting between government representatives and a contingent of Indians regarding their territorial demands, Stanley wrote, "The Indian chiefs were asking the impossible. The half of a continent could not be kept as a buffalo pasture and hunting ground."[26]

The federal government shared Stanley's attitude. Nothing was to delay the progress of the rails. The two railroads and the government would commit whatever resources were necessary to keep the crews moving.

A COORDINATED EFFORT

Although sporadic raids by Indians continued, work on the Union Pacific settled into a routine that involved precise coordination between five specialized crews: surveyors, graders, rail setters, spikers, and tampers. Of these five basic jobs, surveying required the most planning. To accomplish the task, many small surveying groups fanned out across the landscape to record the characteristics of the terrain and report their findings. The surveyor's job was to avoid as many grades as possible, find the shortest route between towns, bridge rivers at the narrowest points, locate the lowest passes through mountain ranges, and avoid the need for tunnels. Often these objectives were incompatible, and the chief surveyor's job was to weigh all factors and come up with a route that was as direct and cost-effective as possible.

After the route was selected and staked, the graders came forward to level and smooth a rail bed. Grading for the Union

Pacific was different from grading for the Central Pacific. Much of the route along the Platte River was subject to flooding, so the rail bed needed to be at least a few feet above the surrounding land. That often meant hauling in soil, and since the rail bed needed to be at least twelve feet wide for a single track and as wide as one hundred feet to accommodate double tracks and sidings, immense amounts of material were often needed. Where a steep hill lay in the path of the railroad, the opposite problem faced the crew as they made a cut into the hill to keep the grade as level as possible. The top of the cut had to be wider than the bottom to prevent the earth from sliding over the tracks. This process sometimes meant removing thousands of cubic feet of rock and dirt—all by hand.

Only the hardiest workers could sustain a long day of moving dirt and rock. Working with basic tools such as shovels, picks, and wheelbarrows put calluses on the men's hands and kept them physically fit. When the going got particularly tough, horse-drawn scrapers helped level the rail bed. If the grading crews encountered hard rock that needed to be leveled, they blasted it loose.

Once the rail bed had been prepared, the next step was to lay the track. However, the Union Pacific's crews once again faced a problem their Central Pacific counterparts did not: lack of timber suitable for ties and bridges. The amount of wood needed was immense, and there was no way of getting around that requirement. The congressionally mandated standards required twenty-five hundred ties per mile regardless of availability of materials.

Finding wood suitable for making ties and building bridges in the Great Plains was nearly impossible. For the most part,

Only the strongest workers were able to endure the long days of moving dirt and rocks.

HELL ON WHEELS

As the Union Pacific moved farther west away from Council Bluffs, the work crews found their pockets bulging with money with nowhere to spend it. Unscrupulous entrepreneurs of the Great Plains saw this as an opportunity to get rich. Known to everyone as "Hell on Wheels," this circus of devious owners of saloons, gambling dens, and bordellos set up their tents and moved west along with the track crews.

These traveling businesses exemplified the Wild West and were operated by the sleazier elements of society. First to find their way were the saloons. Whiskey, the preferred alcoholic drink of the crews, was about ten times the price paid in Omaha. Nonetheless, plenty of patrons were willing to pay the inflated prices. Drinks with names such as Red Dog, Red Cloud, and Red Eye reflected the tone of the saloons.

Next to arrive were the gambling tables, usually operated by the saloon owners. Gambling brought in more money than whiskey did. Once the railroad crews were intoxicated, the card dealers were able to cheat them without being caught. Poker games named High-Low, Mexican Monte, One-eyed Jacks, and Chuck-a-Luck were known to all who entered the saloons. When cheating was suspected, pistols were drawn and fired. Fatal shootings in back alleys were a common occurrence.

Finally there were the brothels. Bands of traveling women followed the railroad crews down the tracks. Far from home and weary of working among thousands of filthy men, the workmen were only too happy to give the women a share of their wages.

John Casement was willing to tolerate Hell on Wheels up to a point. When the night's activities prevented his men from working the next day, he entered the tent town with two hundred armed men and ordered the owners to reduce their operations. When they spat at him, Casement's men opened fire, killing several of the owners. Hell on Wheels was quieter after his visit.

the only trees in the region were groves of spindly cottonwood that grew along riverbanks. Even large cottonwoods were not well suited for railroad ties because their high water content would cause them to rot within a year or two. Durant was aware

of the problem, but he was even more aware that his railroad was behind schedule. Frustrated by the delay, he ordered, without first asking the price, three hundred thousand hardwood ties—enough to carry the rails for the first 120 miles—to be delivered to Omaha. Durant exploded when he saw the bill: $1,350,000. He realized that the railroad could not continue to incur such inflated costs and survive.

The answer to the problem, at least for the short term, was a machine called a Burnettizer. This device was a huge fifty-five-ton cylinder, one hundred feet long and five feet in diameter that could accommodate 250 railroad ties at a time. By creating a vacuum in the cylinder, the Burnettizer sucked the water out of the cells of the wood. Following the extraction of the water, chemicals were injected to give the ties added strength; the ties were then dried.

The Burnettizer saved the Union Pacific from bankruptcy. The cost per tie in the Burnettizer was a mere sixteen cents, which when added to the costs to cut and haul the cottonwood logs was still substantially below the price Durant had paid for the hardwood ties. When he was told that the Burnettized ties would not last as long as the hardwood ties, Durant brushed the warning aside with his usual comment about the need to move the railroad west as fast as possible. As it turned out, Durant would later need to replace all of the cottonwood ties treated in the Burnettizer. In the long run, those "cheaper" ties cost the Union Pacific more than the hardwood ties. Fortunately, once the railroad reached the western boundary of the state of Nebraska, groves of hardwoods better suited for use as ties became available.

With the rails in place, workers measured the gauge for compliance with the required 4 feet, 8½-inch spacing. Spikers, men swinging sledgehammers, drove 6-inch-long iron spikes into the ties to hold the rails in place. Three swings per spike slammed them into place. A half-inch gap between the rail ends provided room for expansion during the summer heat.

Following the spiking of the rails, the tamping crew came in with wagons filled with crushed gravel or sand to be used as ballast to prevent the rails and ties from shifting under the weight of passing trains. Gravel was preferred to sand because it was less likely to be blown away by the wind or washed out by a flash flood, but gravel was also more difficult to find and more expensive to crush and haul. As a result, sand was often used as a substitute for gravel. Crews shoveled the ballast over the ties, completely burying them. Tampers using heavy pieces of wood posts then pounded on the gravel to make sure that it filled all the spaces between ties. Finally, a locomotive ran over the tracks as a final test of gauge and stability.

Under most circumstances, these crews worked smoothly in a well-organized sequence and moved steadily west. As long as things went well, the Union Pacific was receiving sixteen thousand dollars in government bonds plus twenty square miles of federal land for each mile of track. The problem with the procedure was that the Indians continued to oppose the railroad's encroachment on what they considered their own land.

RATTLES OF A DYING CIVILIZATION

In November 1866, following continued attacks against the railroad, General William Tecumseh Sherman, the highest-ranking

Under most circumstances, work on the Union Pacific was well organized as the track progressed steadily west.

general in the West, petitioned the federal government to remove all Indian tribes from the path of the Union Pacific Railroad. In a report to the secretary of war, Sherman wrote:

> This [path] would leave for our people exclusively the use of the wide belt, east and west, between the Platte [River] and the Arkansas [River], in

which lie the two great railroads, and over which pass the bulk of travel to the mountain Territories.[27]

To emphasize the army's commitment to driving the Indians away from the path of the railroad, Sherman ordered the construction of a chain of military forts from the Platte River into Montana along what was known as the Bozeman Trail. The Indians, who had already concluded that the Iron Horse was unmistakably their enemy, watched the building of the forts with dismay, but there was little they could do.

The Union Pacific confirmed the Indians' fears soon enough. Well before the transcontinental railroad was completed, trains began bringing settlers west into the Great Plains. The Union Pacific had not even moved very deeply into Indian territory, but thousands of settlers were already arriving, and small towns sprang up in the wake of the railroad.

Given the irreconcilable interests of whites and Indians, violence was, perhaps, inevitable. And violence was met with violence. In one incident in December 1866,

SCALPING

Native Americans of the plains scalped those they had overcome in hand-to-hand combat. As the Union Pacific Railroad crews worked, the telegraph company followed setting their telegraph lines. The Indians knew that if they cut the wires, the telegraph company would send a crew to make the repairs. One day a band of Cheyenne cut the lines and awaited the telegraph company crew. When the crew arrived to make the repairs, all were immediately killed except William Thompson, who survived the attack. The British journalist Henry Morton Stanley relates this account in his autobiography.

Stanley, later encountered Thompson, who told him that one Cheyenne Indian rode him down "and clubbed me with his rifle. He then took out his knife, stabbed me in the neck, and making a twirl around his fingers with my hair, he commenced sawing and hacking away at my scalp." Feigning death, Thompson knew "enough to keep quiet."

"After what seemed like an hour, my scalp was simply ripped off by the impatient Cheyenne—it just felt as if the whole head was taken off." Lying there dazed and bleeding, he noticed that as the Indian remounted his horse, Thompson's "scalp fell with a plop to the ground." When the Indian rode off, Thompson put his scalp in a pail of water. Stanley noted that "in a pail of water by his side, was his scalp, about nine inches in length and four in width, somewhat resembling a drowned rat." Later Stanley continued the gruesome story, saying that Thompson took his scalp to doctors to "reset the scalp on his head, almost as if it were prairie sod but the painful operation failed, to his disappointment."

Captain William Fetterman, who regarded the Indians as merely temporary impediments to the railroad's progress, openly boasted that he could cut his way through Sioux territory with an army of only eighty men. Fetterman set out with eighty men to rescue a party of Union Pacific's woodcutters who had been captured by a band of Sioux. The Sioux massacred Fetterman and his entire contingent.

During the course of the next two years, 1867 to 1868, many tribes made quick attacks against the railroad crews. Usually the story was the same: The Native Americans would capture and torture the workmen until they died. Scalping was the most common and well-known torture, but stories of skinning men and setting them on fire while still alive were also told. Diaries of workmen tell chilling stories recounting Indian raids against crews operating in the wilderness. One worker recorded this observation in his journal:

> Many and many has been the days that I have proceeded to my duty at the risk of my life. I am haunted by the wild war whoops of the Indians. I have seen them fall before our bullets . . . their day has, however, nearly ended.[28]

Eventually the railroad crews, with their greater supply of men, weapons, and ammunition, gained the upper hand. The Native Americans never had a chance of prevailing against the combined forces of the U.S. government and the Union Pacific. These attacks were, as one American historian noted, "simply the rattle of a [the Indians'] dying civilization."[29]

Congressional committees summoned many railroad executives to testify on a variety of topics after the railroad had been completed. When questioned about the Indians, Grenville Dodge similarly observed that at best, the Indians had only delayed the railroad's work:

> Our Indian troubles commenced in 1864 and lasted until the tracks joined at Promontory. We lost most of our men and stock while building from Fort Kearney to Bitter Creek. At that time every mile of road had to be surveyed, graded, tied, and bridged under military protection. The order to every surveying corps, grading, bridging, and tie outfit was never to run when attacked. All were required to be armed, and I do not know that the order was disobeyed in a single instance, nor did I ever hear that the Indians had driven a party permanently from its work.[30]

Ironically, the Civil War, which had delayed work on the Union Pacific for years by tying up so many potential workers, contributed to the ultimate success of the railroad. Historians note that the small and sporadic raids mounted by the Indians, which killed fifteen or twenty settlers or railroad crew members at a time, meant little to veterans of the Civil War, who had witnessed thousands dying in battle in a single day. And from the standpoint of Union Pacific's directors, the attacks amounted to nothing more than slight financial irritations. Brushing aside the price that both

Indians and Union Pacific work crews would pay in the form of human lives in these skirmishes, the railroad pushed forward.

ACROSS THE ROCKIES

As the rails moved west, another challenge the Union Pacific faced was the Rocky Mountains. The Rockies are a two-thousand-mile chain of rugged mountains that extend from New Mexico north into Canada. Rising as high as thirteen thousand feet in places, the Rockies were a formidable barrier, although not nearly as difficult for the railroad builders as the Sierra Nevada.

Dodge discovered that by following the Snake River in Wyoming, the Union Pacific would avoid high elevations. Better still, once the line was through the Rockies, the stretch between Laramie, Wyoming, and the Utah state line would be relatively flat. According to Dodge, "It almost seems like nature made this great opening in the Rocky Mountains expressly for the passage of a transcontinental railroad."[31] The pass was an obvious choice, and Dodge clearly understood that his crews were by no means the first to discover it, observing, "This route was made by the buffalo, next used by the Indians, then by the fur trades, next by the Mormons, and then by the overland immigration to California and Oregon."[32]

Now, the Union Pacific construction crews made good progress. In November 1867, the men known as the Casement

---

INDIAN NEGOTIATIONS

As raids on the Union Pacific continued, President Andrew Johnson set up a peace commission to discuss the railroad with various Indian tribes. The commission traveled from tribe to tribe with the expressed intention of telling the Indians that the railroads would be built. In September 1867, the commission met with Sioux and Cheyenne. During the meeting, General Ulysses S. Grant delivered this speech, quoted by Stephen E. Ambrose in his book, Nothing Like It in the World.

"This railroad will be built, but if you are damaged [by it] we must pay you in full, and if your young men will interfere the Great Father [the president of the United States], who out of love for you, withheld his soldiers, will let loose his young men, and you will be swept away. We will build iron roads, and you cannot stop the locomotive any more than you can stop the sun or the moon, and you must submit, and do the best you can."

Army approached Cheyenne, Wyoming, five hundred miles from their starting point in Council Bluffs. Still, a shortage of wood plagued them because continued Indian attacks slowed the work of the railroad's loggers. With the onset of winter, the crews stopped work and awaited the spring thaw in Cheyenne.

The Union Pacific could afford to halt work for the winter because by this time, the railroad was actually in the business of moving passengers and freight across the Great Plains. The railroad's rolling stock consisted of fifty-three locomotives, eleven hundred freight cars, ten passenger cars, and dozens of specialty cars for repairs and general services. Better yet, the Union Pacific was now making money from its operations. The company could now boast to its stockholders of profits from passenger tickets and from hauling freight. The railroad not only was proving to be profitable, as it moved west, it also brought with it settlers, houses, fences, prospectors, and towns. What had been the Great American Desert was beginning to blossom.

The winter of 1868 was one of the worst in history, but in April the Union Pacific was again under way. The crews quickly reached the Sherman Summit, which at 8,242 feet was the highest elevation the Union Pacific would reach. With the need to gain elevation came winding track and the need for bridges to span rivers. At Dale Creek, the engineers built the largest of the Union Pacific bridges, 700 feet long and 126 feet above the creek. Once the Rockies had been crossed, the downhill run toward Laramie, Wyoming, went quickly as the crews completed three miles a day.

THE FINAL RUN

Crossing the alkali desert of western Wyoming and Utah, the crews suffered in the summer heat as they worked to lay rails as fast as possible. In spite of the brutal conditions, in the three months between July 21 and October 20, the Casement Army laid 181 miles of track. By this time, the objective was clear: grab as many miles as possible from the Central Pacific, which was now racing across Nevada.

As the Union Pacific's crews crossed the desolate Wyoming landscape toward Utah and the gap between the two railroads closed, more and more newspaper crews moved to the front of the tracks to report on what had become a great race. Not only was the competition exciting, but also the significance of the impending linkage of the two rail lines was apparent to everyone.

In preparation for the final sprint, the Union Pacific approached Brigham Young and the Mormons living in Salt Lake City, in hopes of recruiting additional labor. The Mormons' leader, Brigham Young, was a shrewd businessman who saw the railroad as an important commercial link for his isolated religious enclave. A contract between the Mormons and the Union Pacific was reached, which called for Mormons to work on the railroad construction. In return, Young extracted from the railroad a promise to transport Mormon immigrants to Utah at reduced rates

The Bridge at Dale Creek was the largest of the Union Pacific bridges. It was 700 feet long and 126 feet above the water.

plus a seat for himself on the Union Pacific's board of directors. The agreement added an additional four thousand workers to the Union Pacific's labor force. Young contracted with the Central Pacific in the same manner.

With the additional workers, the remaining few miles to Promontory Summit were quickly laid. Now, for the first time since work on the transcontinental railroad began, none of the crew members or the railroad company owners were in a hurry because the place where the rails would join had been established by law. This fact, however, although comforting to the railroad personnel, did not conceal the continuing sense of urgency within the government to hurry and finish the job.

RENDEZVOUS AT PROMONTORY POINT

The Central Pacific awaited the Union Pacific, working its way through the last few miles of rocky terrain to complete its 1,086 miles from Council Bluffs. While waiting, the Central Pacific began to lay off some of the crews and to send others back up the line to finish spiking loose rails and shoring up hastily built rail beds. The rush to capture as many miles as possible meant that more work was still needed on most of the track to guarantee the safety of the trains.

On the morning of May 6, 1869, a private train departed Sacramento, carrying Governor Leland Stanford, a contingent of other California state officials, and a single golden spike, which would be set as the last spike that would be used to join the two railroads during the ceremony at Promontory Summit. The golden spike was the same size as the iron spikes, but it weighed eighteen ounces and had cost the state of California $360.

On May 8, the unofficial celebration at Promontory, Utah, began with a parade and a cannon blast. A newspaper reporter spotted a Wells Fargo stagecoach pull into Promontory Summit with the last mail run by stagecoach. The reporter was aware that the new technology of the steam-powered railroad was replacing an antiquated, horse-powered system. He filed this story:

> The four old nags [horses] were worn out and the coach showed evidence of long service. The mail matter was de-

The Central Pacific meets the Union Pacific at Promontory Point in Utah. The last spike was driven on May 10, 1869.

livered to the Central Pacific Co., and with that dusty, dilapidated coach and team the old order of things passed away for ever.[33]

On May 10, the official ceremony took place. Little planning had been done because of the remoteness of the dusty town—there were no hotels and few restaurants where visiting dignitaries could sleep or dine. Most of the major figures responsible for the success of the two railroads were absent. The only symbolic event that had been planned well in advance had been the driving of the golden spike. Organizers planned to attach a telegraph wire to the head of the spike so that when it was struck, a signal would travel through the telegraph lines and alert the nation of the railroad's completion.

To make this work smoothly, the hole for the golden spike was drilled in the tie ahead of time so the spike would easily drop in.

Exactly at noon, each railroad brought forward an engine so that the two locomotives sat nose to nose. With photographers present to record the event, leaders of both railroads made brief speeches and Stanford prepared to tap in the golden spike. Wishing to make a good impression before the assembled witnesses, Stanford took a hard swing—and missed. Nonetheless, the telegraph operator quickly relayed the message the nation had been awaiting for five years: "DONE." Photographers recorded the scene, and then friends of Stanford's grabbed the golden spike and hid it in his railroad car for the return trip to Sacramento.

Chapter

6 The Race to Settle the New American Landscape

The race to Promontory Point, which had appeared to be a good old-fashioned competition between two spirited rival companies, was seen quite differently by the government. In reality, one motive behind the construction had always been, in addition to linking California to the eastern states, to secure the last great tract of unsettled territory in America—the Great Plains. At that time, it seemed to some in the federal government that other entities might try to lay claim to large tracts of U.S. territory. It had been only twenty-one years, after all, since the conclusion of the Mexican-American War, and relations with Mexico were still raw. Border skirmishes continued for many years, prompting Washington to encourage Americans to settle the area with the intent of squelching more serious conflicts before they arose.

In addition to securing the new territory, Congress wanted to keep America's factories working. To accomplish this objective, factories needed to be supplied with raw materials, and workers and their families needed to be fed. The natural resources of the nation's interior promised to provide raw materials for manufacturing as well as food for the growing populations of the cities. The only way to move the massive amounts of required natural resources was by railroad. Just as the flow of resources from the Great Plains to industrial cities could fuel American industry, the flow of modern machinery and

Molten steel is ladled into molds. Raw materials and natural resources for factories could only be transported by railroad.

manufactured household goods back to the farms and small towns of the nation's midsection could fuel growth in agriculture and mining.

Only the railroads would be able to provide the rolling stock large enough to move heavy farm and mining machinery to the towns throughout the Midwest at affordable prices. In the great scheme for America's future, the transcontinental railroad played a pivotal role in the transportation cycle of natural resources and manufactured products.

SAN FRANCISCO TO NEW YORK: EIGHT DAYS

The completion of the transcontinental railroad impacted the general population in many significant ways, but none more so than the time it saved traveling between the two coasts. Within one week of the railroad's completion, regularly scheduled train service began, with one train running per day in each direction. The roughly eighteen hundred miles of railroad between Council Bluffs and Sacramento was a single track, which meant that trains had to pull over to sidings when they approached one another, and that slowed the journey considerably. Still, the time to make the trip between Council Bluffs and Sacramento was just four and one-half days. For travelers going all the way from San Francisco to New York, the trip was just under eight days. The average speed of the trains, including all stops at stations and for water and coal, was eighteen miles per hour. Compared to the

one-half mile per hour average speed of the covered wagons or the four miles per hour of the stagecoaches, the trains were considered speedy. Compared to the six month's travel time required by ships going around the tip of South America or across the Isthmus of Panama, the eight days by train was nothing short of a miracle. Moreover, the accommodations were far more comfortable. Even the mail would make the trip faster and much cheaper than either the stagecoach or the famed Pony Express.

Although the rail journey across the country was relatively cheap and fast, a ticket still represented about one month's wages for the average traveler. People of means paid one hundred dollars for a first-class ticket that enabled them to stretch out and sleep on padded couches. Second-class passengers paid eighty dollars for comfortable but basic seats, and third-class travelers paid forty dollars to sit tightly packed on wood benches. Still, in the first year of operation, 150,000 passengers made the cross-country trip.

IMMIGRANTS

Although a small number of hearty pioneers had begun settling the Great Plains in the years before the transcontinental railroad was completed, their numbers were few compared to the droves that came once the railroad made the plains accessible. The first to take the trains were Americans seeking farmland just as their ancestors had done coming to the East Coast from Europe.

First-class passengers enjoy their trip from New York to San Francisco.

The railroad companies also played a pivotal role in attracting new immigrants to America. Railroads sent out advertisements to hundreds of European newspapers in which they offered to sell the thousands of acres of federal land they had received for each mile of track laid. These advertisements, coupled with word-of-mouth stories about cheap land, attracted millions of Europeans who wished to become a part of the American adventure.

In retrospect, it is difficult to overestimate the impact that this new wave of immigration had on American society. Historian Judith Clark notes:

In fact, immigration could perhaps be counted the single most important factor in social change of the period. Between 1860 and 1890, 10 million

Europeans arrived in the United States, where they hoped to find economic opportunity, enjoy religious freedom or discover the other assurances promised by democratic government. The arrival of these immigrant groups made a sustained impact on America, providing a steady supply of inexpensive labor and creating instant markets for food, housing, and clothing.[34]

After immigrants disembarked from their boats in New York City and were cleared by immigration officers, most settled in large industrial cities. They settled in ethnic neighborhoods with names such as Little Italy, German Town, and Russian Hill, where their native languages were spoken and they were reunited with family and friends. These immigrants typically found low-income work in restaurants, factories, and cleaning establishments without ever seeing the new western territory opened by the railroads. In this sense, many fared no better than their ancestors who had immigrated to America one hundred years earlier.

Although the majority of the immigrants settled in cities in the East, those who had already purchased railroad land or had farming experience climbed aboard trains and headed west. The influx of immigrants and Americans to the newly opened territories between 1870 and 1880, the ten-year period that followed the completion of the transcontinental railroad, was extraordinary. South Dakota's population increased from 11,000 to 98,000, Colorado's from 40,000 to 194,000, and Nebraska's from 123,000 to 452,000.

THE NEW AMERICAN LANDSCAPE

Communities in what had been the Great American Desert began with one or two adventurous families. As communities of farmers grew, tradespeople soon followed to support everyone's needs. As this sequence of events repeated itself hundreds of times over the vast western reaches opened by the railroads, the appearance of the American landscape changed dramatically.

Although the transcontinental railroad began as a single line, the government intended to expand it as quickly as possible. The U.S. government continued paying the railroads to lay track, and by 1884, several rail lines stretched across the South from several major cities such as Atlanta and New Orleans, leading to Los Angeles. Several more lines linked northern cities such as Chicago and St. Louis with Seattle and Portland. These lines running east and west were quickly connected by smaller lines running north and south, creating a grid of rails that brought most new farms and towns within, at most, a two-day trip to a major city.

Immigrants were not the only ones to take advantage of the trains; Americans were also climbing aboard to build new lives. To speed the process of populating the new territory, Congress had passed the Homestead Act of 1862 to encourage thousands of Americans to leave the eastern states for new lives in the Great Plains. This law provided 160 acres of land at no cost to American citizens willing to farm it for at least five years. Because of the Civil War and the difficulty of traveling to remote parcels within Indian territories, this incentive had little initial impact. Twenty years later, however, the railroads and the Homestead Act did more to populate the Great Plains than any other factor.

The increasing population changed the look of the Great Plains from one of wide-open grasslands and arid landscapes to a scattering of small towns and farms. At first, there were only a few hundred new

IMMIGRANT WOMEN

The life of the immigrant family often involved a difficult struggle for survival on the prairie. The role that women played was no easier than that of men. These insights were compiled by sociologist Dr. JoAnn Hanson-Stone, writing for the Institute of Migration website, based on excerpts written by Finnish women who settled with their husbands and families in Wisconsin and Minnesota.

"The farmer worked hard, but his wife worked even harder. She did the housework, cared for the children, prepared the meals, helped to care for the cattle, pigs, sheep and chickens; milked the cows, churned the butter, did the canning in summer and fall, prepared cheese, carded and spun the wool [they brought their spinning wheels and looms], wove cloth, dyed it with homemade dyes, knitted and sewed clothing, mended mittens and socks. On occasion she pitched in and helped to rake hay and bind the grain after it had been cut. . . . She bore children year after year; she cared for the sick when her home was struck by disease.

She [a specific Finnish woman] bore thirteen children, ten growing to adulthood; for forty years she was the region's only midwife, making 103 safe deliveries. When her husband worked at distant logging camps, she took charge of the farm; she hitched the horse, plowed and harrowed, sowed seed by hand from a dishpan; she milked the cows and nursed the ailing stock. She tanned hides and made footwear, spun wool and knitted garments. She hauled food supplies from the nearest store, a round-trip journey requiring three days. She kept the farmhouse in repair, raised the chimney, and found the time to help the neighbors; once she rescued a child from a 28-foot well. She felt no sense of being a heroine, wrote a reporter, but because she had versatile ability and unquenchable energy, she lived up to the standards of that day. These people had to work hard, do those things, or go under."

towns, but by the end of the nineteenth century, thousands of towns and cities dotted the map. As the settlers brought by the railroads planted their crops, the landscape changed from the grays and browns of the native vegetation to the greens and golds of grains and other crops.

TOWNS AND CITIES

In addition to changing the landscape, the newly created railroad network spurred and then shaped the growth of America's towns and cities. Most major towns throughout the Great Plains sprouted along the railroad lines. They were called "railroad towns" because the railroads were the largest employers and because farmers and ranchers mostly came to town to ship their crops and cattle and to pick up machinery and tools shipped to them from eastern fac-

tories. These towns catered to the needs of the farmers by providing equipment dealers and mechanics, hardware stores, banks, doctors, schools, churches, and sometimes a newspaper. Travelers approaching these towns could see their landmarks from miles away—church steeples as well as tall silos that stored millions of bushels of grain. In addition to the small downtown area surrounding the railroad depot, the larger towns featured stockyards that held thousands of head of cattle awaiting shipment to slaughterhouses in the East.

Where two or more rail lines intersected, small towns often grew into major transportation hubs. Processing plants sprang up because so many food products funneled into these railroad hubs. Food processing plants took grains, vegetables, and cattle and converted them into boxed and wrapped food for purchase by families and restaurants in distant cities.

Railroad towns sprang up throughout the Great Plains. They got their name partly because the railroads were the largest employers.

GEORGE PULLMAN

As the railroads spread across America, a New Yorker by the name of George Pullman saw an opportunity to provide more comfortable accommodations for weary travelers crossing great distances. In 1867, Pullman created the Pullman Palace Car Company to manufacture sleeping and dining cars.

Known during the latter half of the nineteenth century as "rolling hotels," Pullman cars offered fine dining, barbers, hairdressers and manicurists, baths, and even libraries with the latest books and magazines. Most famous of the various types of cars were the sleeping cars, which featured wood-paneled sleeping compartments that were about forty square feet, with either a single bed or upper and lower beds for double occupancy. Each compartment included hot and cold water and overhead luggage racks. They were prized for their interior elegance of lacquered woods, polished brass, and beautiful lamps and drapes.

When the company's fortunes declined in 1894, Pullman slashed workers' pay but neglected to lower the cost of rent and groceries that he charged them in the Pullman Company town. Pullman had built this town for all of his employees to live in because he believed it would be a decent place for them and because he could control it as he wished. A delegation of workers who went to ask Pullman to lower costs was fired. This prompted the workers to go on strike. The Pullman strike spread to the entire railroad. To get the railroads running again, President Grover Cleveland sent federal troops, which severely injured many Pullman strikers. The workers finally went back to work, but Pullman was so hated that when he died in 1897, his heirs placed his coffin in a block of concrete, fearing someone might try to steal his body and publicly burn it.

Following Pullman's death, the company recovered and continued manufacturing its luxury cars. In 1907, the wood cars transitioned to steel, and the increase in demand for thousands of steel cars resulted in an expansion of the company to ten thousand employees by 1917. Success continued until a preference for jet plane travel forced the company to close in 1969.

Metropolitan centers such as Topeka, Kansas; Lincoln, Nebraska; and Kansas City, Missouri, in large measure owe their present-day stature to the transcontinental railroad. Thanks to the railroad, the vast expanse that was once named the Great American Desert by early nineteenth-century pioneers was appropriately renamed America's Bread Basket.

FEEDING AMERICA

Just as nobody actually foresaw the contribution the American industrial revolution would make to the transcontinental railroad, nobody foresaw how the railroad would help America replace England as the leading industrialized nation in the world. Whether anyone was aware of it or not, it was America's farmers, supported by the railroad, who made this possible.

If the transcontinental railroad made farming possible in much of the country, that hardly meant that life was easy for those new farmers. Before crops could be planted, the soil had to be prepared. The biggest jobs were removing large rocks, draining swamps, and in some northern areas, cutting down trees and digging out the stumps. The first farmers to settle this land had to contend with sod—hard soil clumps held together by thickly matted grass roots. Only after the sod had been plowed several times to turn and break up the grassy clumps was it suitable for planting. The early pioneering families therefore acquired the name, "Sod Busters." First-year farmers lived in sod houses and often planted no more than two acres of land to feed their families.

If, however, farmers survived the first two or three years, their simple needs became more complicated. The two acres under cultivation often grew to twenty acres and then fifty. As farms prospered and grew, the need for more efficient farm equipment spurred industry to produce larger and more sophisticated farming implements.

Fortunately for the farmers, America's manufacturers were developing heavier machinery to help crop production. However, as machinery grew in size, the only transportation system capable of accommodating it was the railroad. To help both the farmers and the manufacturers, the railroads constructed larger flatcars to accommodate the heavy equipment. The multidisk John Deere plows that turned and broke up the sod and the McCormick mechanized reapers that cut crops such as wheat, barley, oats, and flax could fit on new flatcars. Thanks to the railroads, a steam-powered tractor manufactured in Moline, Illinois, could be delivered by flatcar to Swedish immigrant farmers in Braddock, North Dakota, within two days.

Because of the growth of the railroads and of industry, farming became so successful that between 1860 and 1890, the amount of farmland more than doubled, increasing from 400 million to 880 million acres. During this same period, farm production became so efficient that for the first time, farms produced more food than Americans could consume. This boost was just what big industrial cities needed to meet the needs of the growing numbers of factory workers.

Transporting food from rural America to the big cities was just as important as transporting heavy farm equipment. To move large volumes long distances, the railroad designed special grain cars that could be coupled together and pulled by a single engine. In 1884 economist David Wells expressed the value of shipping by rail:

Farming equipment such as this multidisk John Deere plow could be transported easily on the railroad.

[A ton of goods] can now be carried on the best managed railroads for a distance of a mile, for a sum so small that outside of China it would be difficult to find a coin of equivalent value to give a boy as a reward for carrying an ounce package across the street.[35]

Fruits and vegetables, however, could not stay fresh as long as grains. To meet the need to keep produce fresh, the railroads offered refrigerator cars—specially constructed double-walled boxcars. The space between the two walls held several hundred-pound blocks of ice, which kept the contents of the cars cool. For the first time, residents in the East and Midwest could

enjoy vegetables and fruits from California and dairy products from the Willamette Valley in Oregon. Moreover, produce that midwesterners could grow only for themselves in the summer was now available in the winter, shipped from where it grew during California's mild winters.

RANCHES

Just as farmers came to rely on the railroads to ship their products, so, too, did ranchers come to depend on the railroads to ship their herds to market. Initially, cattle ranchers allowed their cattle to graze on the open range throughout Texas, Oklahoma, and Colorado. This practice made it possible for some ranchers who owned no land to own thousands of head of cattle. Cowboys followed these roaming herds, protecting them from predators, branding them for identification purposes, and driving them hundreds of miles to market.

The problem with driving cattle to market was that the animals suffered significant weight loss en route, translating into

THE AMERICAN HOBO

Not everyone who rode the railroads did so legally. As the rails fanned out across America, many young men called hobos became part of railroad history. Hobos, from the term "hoe boys," were originally men who would travel between towns hoeing fields in return for food and a dry place to sleep. Since they rarely had much money, they learned the art of jumping on freight cars as the trains made their way across the land.

This tradition began at the end of the Civil War while men were looking for work. Hobos were some of the earliest migrant workers. Catching a ride on a freight train—called "flipping"—was illegal, and if the boys were caught by a railroad agent, they were tossed off the train at the next stop. Flipping was also dangerous. Some who attempted to flip a moving train slipped while making their jump and fell under the wheels. Once on a train, hobos hid among the cattle, coal, or whatever freight the train was pulling. Around the end of the nineteenth century, an estimated 1 million hobos were riding the rails.

Over time, a rich folklore grew up around the American hobo. Country and western songwriters such as Woody Guthrie, Johnny Cash, Elizabeth Cotten, and Doc Watson wrote songs about the antics of the hobos who rode the rails from the beginning of the twentieth century until the end of the Great Depression. Some of them had colorful nicknames such as Fry Pan Jack, Box Car Willie, and Frisco Jack. American novelists also peppered their writings with stories of these drifters who moved from place to place on the trains, trying to find work. During the depression, an estimated 250,000 hobos, mostly teenagers, rode the rails working for food.

Although few hobos still ride the rails, they have played an interesting role in the history of railroading. To a great degree, this part of the American experience ended after World War II when the economy finally recovered from the depression. Nonetheless, the history of the American hobo continues to be told in movies, books, and songs.

less money for the rancher once the cows reached the slaughterhouses. Thanks to the railroads, cattle arrived at the slaughterhouses heavier than they would have been had they walked. As a result, ranchers earned more money even though they had to pay to ship their herds.

During the late 1860s and early 1870s, the railroads came to the aid of ranchers in another way. Overgrazing and a shortage of rainfall combined to decrease the grasslands in the Southwest. This sudden shortage of grass forced ranchers to feed their cattle a mixture of grains as a supplement. The railroads were able to deliver carloads of corn, oats, and other grains for the herds. Owners of large ranches arranged for trains to stop at their ranches for delivery or even built their own short spur lines to avoid the need for using horses and wagons for transferring the feed. In large measure, then, the railroads helped ranchers maintain their way of life.

MINES

Although the farms and ranches fed the industrial workforce, the mines provided the raw materials needed to run the factories. Mine owners in all of the western states realized that the transcontinental railroad would make large-scale mining feasible by linking them with the industries that used their minerals. Thanks to the railroads, vast quantities of iron ore flowed from dozens of small mining towns in Arizona, Nevada, and Colorado. Most mines could never have

existed without the railroads, since their remote locations made the cost of transporting minerals (other than small amounts of gold or silver) by horse or mule extremely high.

The railroads worked to accommodate the needs of the miners just as they had for farmers and ranchers. Specially designed cars were developed, allowing for faster loading and unloading of ore. The railroads developed conveyor belts at railroad yards for fast loading of ore cars. They also developed bins on ore cars that tipped to the side for fast unloading. As the cost to transport minerals fell, more mines opened to supply the factories and iron mills that were producing the machines that were transforming America into an industrial powerhouse.

THE VANISHING FRONTIER

By the early twentieth century, a mere fifty years following the completion of the transcontinental railroad, the American frontier had vanished. Barbed wire, roads, and railroad tracks put an end to the idea that one could settle on and claim seemingly unoccupied land.

The open spaces of the West that Lewis and Clark described could be found only with great difficulty, having given way to tens of thousands of small farms separated by barbed wire fences, hundreds of factories and mills, railroad lines, and flourishing cities. What came to be known as the closing of the American frontier did not go unnoticed, however.

DODGE CITY

Few cities in America captured the flavor of the Wild West, as Dodge City, Kansas. In its early years before the railroads, Dodge was one of many pioneer towns along the legendary Santa Fe Trail, which carried more than five thousand covered wagons a year from Independence, Missouri, to Santa Fe, New Mexico. Once the railroad appeared, however, families moved into the area, ending the lawless reputation of this legendary Wild West town.

Dodge City began as Fort Dodge in 1865 to protect wagon trains from Indian attacks. Six years later, Dodge became a stopping place and trade center for buffalo hunters and travelers. Although Dodge began as a fort, the city grew away from the fort and soon became a town known for lawless activities that the government could not control. Lacking a sheriff, Dodge began to acquire its reputation as a lawless, gunslinging town that attracted many gunfighters willing to test their skills. So many men died in gunfights that the Old West slogan, "dying with their boots on," originated here. The local cemetery, Boot Hill, took its name from those who died with their boots on.

When the railroad arrived in 1880 and the cattle drives passed into history, Dodge City's mystique as a Wild West town ended. The railroad brought legitimate businesses and families, which finally forced the city to hire a series of famous lawmen to take control of the city away from the gunslingers. The first in a long history of Wild West lawmen included Wyatt Earp, William "Bat" Masterson, and Bill Tilghman.

To gain control of the city, these lawmen limited the carrying of guns to the south side of the railroad tracks, where they would not go. The south side of town, known as "the wrong side of the tracks," became a haven for every imaginable type of vice. Gradually, as the town prospered, however, this part of town faded into history.

Some Americans living in the eastern states were eager to take the train west to see the Indians and the buffalo herds that they read about in the popular literature of the day. Eager to make money from these adventure seekers, the railroads carried thousands to see the places where the Indians had once lived and some of the battle sites where they had died. Some railroads specialized in buffalo safaris, which allowed hunters to kill buffalo from their train cars. Hotels and restaurants sprang up along the rail lines to provide comfortable accommodations for all of these travelers.

During the latter half of the nineteenth century, the West also developed a mystique as a lawless land where gunslingers ruled. A few of these frontier towns—such as Dodge City and Tombstone—developed reputations as places where gunfighters such as Billy the Kid, Butch Cassidy, Doc Holliday, and Wyatt Earp would routinely confront one another.

Regardless of the truth of the stories about what was known as the Wild West, the arrival of the railroads in these remote regions brought with it a civilizing influence. As the railroads brought more and more farmers, ranchers, and miners who built homes and raised families, the Wild West slipped away and became the stuff of legends.

7 Troubling Consequences

The completion of the transcontinental railroad achieved the primary objective of securing America's manifest destiny. The nation was at last linked coast to coast and border to border by rails that transported Americans and immigrants to thousands of new towns and cities. Within twenty-five years of the completion of the transcontinental railroad, all who had supported its completion took pride in its success. There was good reason to be proud of the achievement that many historians call one of the most significant in America's history.

Accompanying this magnificent triumph, however, were many consequences that President Lincoln could not have foreseen when he signed the Railroad Act of 1862. The completion of the railroad at Promontory Summit was quickly eclipsed by many troubling events that followed. Although nearly everyone had benefited in one way or another from the grid of railroads fanning out across the West, others experienced great disillusionment and bitterness. No single group suffered more grievously from the building of the transcontinental railroad than the American Indian.

RAILS OF DEATH

The transcontinental railroad, despite being but a single track, literally and figuratively ripped apart the Indians' way of life. By the time the railroad was completed, both whites and Indians clearly saw that their two cultures could not co-exist. If white settlers were going to farm the Great Plains, mine the deserts and mountains, herd cattle across the grass-lands, and connect all of these far-flung lands with a network of rails, then there could be no room for the nomadic Indians who pursued the herds of buffalo. Furthermore, if whites were going to insist upon claiming the land, dividing it into small parcels that could be bought and sold, and protecting it from those who sought to cross it, there could be no place for the Indians who had no tradition of land ownership or private property.

Of all the points of conflict between the two cultures, the issue of the buffalo was the most significant. Indispensable to the livelihood of Indians, these huge animals were even more important than the horse. Buffalo were the Indians' most valuable source—sometimes their only source—of food, clothing, shelter, warmth, tools, and spirituality. The nomadic Indian tribes moved back and forth across the Great Plains, following the herds and organizing their lives and religion around the hunt. For perhaps a decade or two, the Indians might have been able to tolerate the influx of settlers that the railroads brought, had it not disturbed the grazing habits of the buffalo that they depended on.

Herds of thousands of buffalo must migrate over vast tracts of grassland to survive. Weighing over a ton, each animal consumes enormous amounts of grass each day. As they eat the grass, the buffalo must continue moving to find new grazing lands. When the buffalo first encountered the rails, they refused to cross them. As if confronting a wall, they turned around and tried to graze on the grassland they had just passed through. Deprived of adequate nourishment, many starved during the harsh winters of the plains.

As additional rail lines were added, the buffalo and the Indians became trapped between the rails as the grazing lands decreased in size. The inevitable demise of the herds and the Indians was predicted in 1872 when the U.S. commissioner of Indian affairs, Ely S. Parker, observed: "The progress on the Northern Pacific railroad will of itself leave the ninety thousand Indians ranging between the transcontinental lines as incapable of resisting the Government as are the Indians of New York or Massachusetts."[36]

Eventually, herds bolted across the railroad tracks and destroyed them by pulverizing the wood ties and scattering the gravel ballast. To protect railroad property, the railroad companies hired buffalo hunters to kill as many animals as possible. Although the number killed by the railroad marksmen is widely disputed, large herds were unquestionably obliterated. By the end of the 1870s, the railroad hunters had been joined by cattlemen and sportsmen who hunted the buffalo close to extinction.

Indians attack a buffalo herd. White settlers left no room for the nomadic tribes who hunted the animals.

Secondary to the buffalo problem for the Indians was the federal authorities' refusal to interfere on behalf of the Indians when their lands were seized by whites flooding into Indian lands. In fact, federal troops often participated in the seizures. The government's attitude was nothing new. In a speech to Congress in 1866, President Andrew Johnson had addressed the Native American issue by asserting, "If the savage resists, civilization, with the Ten Commandments in one hand and the sword in the other, demand his immediate extermination."[37]

UNFORESEEN PROBLEMS

Although Native Americans opposed the rails from the start, they were shortly

---

GRASSHOPPERS TOO MANY TO KILL

The U.S. government routinely broke treaties they had signed with many Indian tribes guaranteeing them open tracts of land. As their guaranteed land was gradually taken away from them, the government created reservations as places to isolate the Indians. Reservations proved unsuitable for Indians' migratory lives, and the land chosen for their reservations was generally of poor quality. In addition to these realities, they understood that the white civilization had taken everything from them. These terrible conditions, coupled with the mass extermination of the buffalo, quickly led to declining standards of living for the Indians. Starvation on reservations, freezing winters without adequate shelter, and a broken spirit over lost traditional hunting lands left them with inconsolable sadness. In his book, A Sunday Between Wars, *Ben Maddow recounts the sadness that a chief of the Sisseton tribe expressed.*

"I remember the big council of fire when we signed away our first land. At that time, the country was full of buffalo and when I was 20 summers [years old] I killed a cow and calf with one arrow. Then came swarms of grasshopper that ate up all the grass for four seasons. Then bones of the buffalo became white on the hillsides and they were poor and of little meat. Then the grasshoppers turned into white men and killed off all the buffalo that did not starve. This made great changes to the Indians. He could eat the buffalo and the grasshoppers, but he could not eat the white man. So we had to sell off more of our land to the great father at Washington [the federal government] for meat and blankets."

---

joined by whites who had previously favored the construction of rail lines. When the transcontinental railroad was completed, newspaper editors and politicians proclaimed it one of the greatest engineering achievements of all time. These boosters also fed the perception that the quality of construction was the highest possible and that the rails were perfectly safe. Yet, shortly after the completion of the railroad, the truth about shoddy construction and dangerous working conditions began to emerge.

Many of the shortcuts had been taken to save the railroads money. The most pronounced examples on the Union Pacific's part included such practices as using sand instead of heavy gravel for rail ballast and using soft cottonwood instead of hardwood for ties. Much to the shock and surprise of most Americans, many miles of rail as well as numerous bridges would need to be replaced. The public would pay for these a second time through higher passenger and freight costs.

Within one year of the ceremonious linking of the Union Pacific and Central Pacific at Promontory Summit, travelers began complaining about delays and even train wrecks resulting from poor construction. Many stories of accidents and close brushes with death began emerging, such as this story from a traveler in 1869:

> A bridge over Bitter Creek, just east of Green River, built upon abutments of soft sandstone, crumbled away under our train precipitating the engine, tender [coal car], and express car into the creek. . . . One passenger was killed

and several more or less injured. . . . The bridge had been examined the previous day and was pronounced unsafe. . . . The unanimous decision is that it was criminal to try and cross.[38]

Isaac Morris, a government examiner of the Union Pacific, agreed that the track was in terrible condition. After investigating the ties, he said, "No attention appears to have been paid to regularity of distance between the ties, they vary from fifteen to twenty-six inches. . . . They are of soft white pine."[39] Morris believed that the Union Pacific Railroad was so poorly constructed that he recommended that Congress withhold final payments to it.

In addition to the dangers that the substandard construction created, incidents of injury and death to railroad employees were alarmingly high. Train workers had the highest incidence of injury and death of any profession. These crews had to walk between two moving cars where one slip meant certain death. Accidents while manually coupling and uncoupling cars left many workers missing a hand or fingers. Men stoking the fires aboard the engines frequently suffered severe burns.

Historian Ben Maddow, in his book *A Sunday Between Wars*, cites these chilling railroad statistics:

> Between 1890 and 1917, there were 72,000 railroad employees killed and nearly 2,000,000 injured, and these only on the trains and the tracks themselves, not in the railway repair shops and roundhouses, which counted a total of 237,000 injured and 158,000 killed. These are catastrophic losses,

THE BATTLE OF THE LITTLE BIGHORN

In 1873, when gold was discovered on the Sioux reservation in the Black Hills of South Dakota, thousands of miners trespassed across Indian lands on their way to the gold fields. The Soo Line, one of many small railroads that developed following the completion of the transcontinental railroad, saw an opportunity to transport the miners. Within a year, the Soo Line received permission to extend its rails from the main east-west transcontinental railroad lines north into the Dakotas where miners were registering claims. Angered by these events, the Sioux rallied around their leaders, Sitting Bull and Crazy Horse, and began attacking and killing railroad workers and miners. Following three years of skirmishes that left many dead, the U.S. government finally ordered three regiments of the Seventh Cavalry to proceed to the territory to crush the Sioux. In the summer of 1876, Colonel George Armstrong Custer, with about 255 cavalry, entered the area near the Little Bighorn River in search of Sioux warriors. On the morning of June 25, Custer engaged a large force of Sioux, which massacred his entire regiment. Historian Greg Michno, writing for the June 1996 edition of Wild West *magazine, provides these two eyewitness accounts. The first describes the reaction of the Indians when learning of Custer's approach; the second describes the battle as told by the Indians.*

"Back in the village the news [of Custer's approach] caused havoc. Other women were caught unaware in the middle of their chores. Pretty White Buffalo, Hunkpapa wife of Spotted Horn Bull, was preparing a buffalo meat stew for her brother and had no thoughts of a fight that day. The 13-year-old Oglala Lakota Black Elk was with some other boys, swimming and playing in the waters of the Greasy Grass [the Little Big Horn], when he heard the criers run by with the news. Even the warriors, usually so alert, were caught unprepared."

"'Some of the soldiers broke through the Indians and ran for the ravine,' said Red Hawk, 'but all were killed without getting into it.' The Oglala Fears Nothing [an Indian name] saw them make a break through a narrow gap in the Indian line, but the warriors ran them down and killed them with war clubs. Rain in the Face [a Sioux chief] saw some flee, while another group stayed together at the head of a little ravine, where they fought bravely before they were cut to pieces. Rain had always thought the white men were cowards, but this fight changed his mind. 'I had great respect for them after this day,' he said."

certainly far greater than all the battle casualities of all the Indian wars put together. And passenger deaths and injuries over the same period were roughly as great, with total casualities over 212,000. There is no doubt that the American railroad system, built with such furious energy, was, by any human standards, unsafe at any price particularly for the crews. [40]

THE CRÉDIT MOBILIER SCANDAL

The greatest scandal, however, to emerge from the building of the transcontinental railroad had nothing to do with rails or locomotives or any of the engineering standards in the Railroad Act of 1862. It related to the Union Pacific's finances and involved officers of the company as well as a number of congressional leaders.

Shoddy construction of the railroad caused train wrecks soon after its completion.

The two men principally responsible for the scandal were Thomas Durant, president of the Union Pacific, and Oakes Ames, a congressman from Massachusetts and major stockholder in the Union Pacific. Durant, along with several other large Union Pacific stockholders, purchased a construction company in 1863 and then changed its name to Crédit Mobilier. This construction company sold tools and construction materials in large quantities.

As the railroad crews began to lay track, the Union Pacific entered into a contract with Crédit Mobilier to provide most of the needed tools and materials at prices far higher than those that competing construction companies charged. The owners of the Union Pacific were, in effect, doing business with themselves. Charles Francis Adams, a member of the Massachusetts Board of Railroad Commissioners, published an article dealing with the scandal called "The Pacific Railroad Ring," in which he observed that "they [members of Crédit Mobilier] are ever ubiquitous; they receive money into one hand as a corporation and pay it into the other as a contractor."[41] This deception was kept a secret from the government and most of the people associated with the Union Pacific. Crédit Mobilier charged more than $94 million for construction that actually cost only $44 million. Durant, Ames, and several large stockholders made millions of dollars from this scheme as a result.

This illegal activity was not discovered until the transcontinental railroad had been completed. Suspicions about the fi-

Oakes Ames was one of the Crédit Mobilier stockholders who made millions of dollars from the construction scandal.

nancial dealing between Durant and Ames led to congressional investigations. Ames attempted to limit the investigation by bribing fellow congressmen with Crédit Mobilier stock. Despite Ames's efforts, the scandal became widely publicized, and the public outcry was so great that Crédit Mobilier's operations were halted and the Union Pacific Railroad stripped of many of its assets. The Union Pacific quickly became debt-ridden, and the political careers of many congressional leaders implicated in the scandal were ruined.

This scale of unethical business practices had never occurred before. Small scandals, to be sure, had surfaced before the Crédit Mobilier disgrace, but America's fascination with the railroads quickly gave way to suspicion of the relationship between big business and government. Historian Stephen Ambrose believes that what mattered about this scandal was

> that money that flowed from the Union Pacific into the Crédit Mobilier and what was done with it—which wasn't to pay the contractors, or the subcontractors, or the laborers who had gotten the railroad from Omaha to the Utah border—was further enriching a relatively few already wealthy men who milked the corporation, the government, and ultimately the people for their fat and ill-gotten profits.[42]

EXCESSIVE PROFITS

America's enthusiasm for the railroad dimmed surprisingly fast, in part because of disillusionment brought on by numerous scandals over shoddy workmanship and financial misdealing. A cynicism grew among many working-class Americans who believed that the railroads were built by the blood and sweat of common workers while the big profits went to the wealthy financiers and company stockholders. Suspicion of big business in general and the railroad in particular had been a part of America's thinking for many years. American essayist and philosopher Henry David Thoreau expressed this notion in 1854:

> We do not ride on the railroad; it rides upon us. Did you ever think what those sleepers [ties] are that underlie

the railroad? Each one is a man, an Irishman, or a Yankee man. The rails are laid on them, and they are covered with sand, and the cars run smoothly over them. They are sound sleepers, I assure you. And every few years a new lot is laid down and run over; so that, if some have the pleasure of riding on a rail, others have the misfortune to be ridden upon.[43]

The enormous profits that the railroad financiers and managers were making became another social concern. All of the Big Four became multimillionaires as a result of their investments in the Central Pacific. Although these people had taken some risk in making this investment in a project that could have failed completely, many observers believed that their profits were excessive and were a result of inadequate government oversight. The issue of excessive profits hinged on the fact that both railroads were paid in cash as well as land for every mile of track. Historians Samuel Eliot Morison and Henry Steele Commager have noted: "The lands granted to both the Union Pacific and the Central Pacific yielded enough to have covered all legitimate costs of building these roads."[44] Another twentieth-century historian, Fred Shannon, notes: "The half billion dollars in land alone to the land grant railroads was worth more than the railroads were when they were built."[45]

Following the completion of the first transcontinental rail line, the government continued to promote the building of railroads. As a result, by 1893, in addition to four transcontinental railroads, dozens of lines wove a web of rails through the heartland of America. The number of miles of track in America in 1869, at the completion of the first transcontinental railroad, was 47,000. Ten years later it had more than doubled to 116,000 miles, and by 1890 it had nearly doubled again to a phenomenal 208,000 miles. Rather than

THE CHINESE EXCLUSION ACT

The Chinese who built the railroad for the Central Pacific were not well received by Americans after they had completed the transcontinental railroad. The Chinese were only grudgingly incorporated into American culture, and in many cases, they were not welcome in cities. California's growing prosperity prompted many white workers from the East Coast and Midwest to migrate in search of jobs, which placed them in direct competition with Chinese workers. The labor competition, as well as the willingness of the Chinese to work for lower wages, prompted accusations of a Chinese labor monopoly, which led to an increase in anti-Chinese sentiment and violence.

Several severe race riots occurred in western cities including Rock Springs, Wyoming, where coal miners killed twenty-eight Chinese miners who refused to join a strike. In Los Angeles in 1871, a riot erupted in Chinatown that brought the police as well as armed white citizens. Vigilante groups made their way through Chinatown, shooting at any Chinese they could find and even lynching a few young innocent Chinese men.

Finally, in 1882, responding to pressure from western states, Congress passed the Chinese Exclusion Act, which banned all Chinese laborers, except for teachers and diplomats, from entering the United States. Chinese people born in the United States and their families were allowed to remain. This act was principally designed to prevent an excess of cheap labor. Within the year, emigration from China dropped from forty thousand in 1881 to just twenty-three in 1882.

Although civic groups primarily in San Francisco objected to the act in defense of the hardworking Chinese, rising unemployment among white Americans, coupled with cultural differences such as language, hairstyle, and religion, forced the legislation through Congress.

The Chinese Exclusion Act was the first law to prohibit the immigration of a particular race or nationality of people to the United States. Despite the hardship this law placed on local Chinese populations, it was not repealed until 1948.

rejoicing over this expansion, however, a public outcry arose because many of these miles of track were unnecessary.

Often, the new lines were built solely for the profit that could be made from constructing miles of unneeded track. Railroad companies in the West commonly built more than one set of rails to the same town, and competing railroads sometimes built parallel tracks only a few miles apart. Another trick the railroads used to collect extra money from the government was to choose routes that were many miles longer than necessary. Although many miles of track were unnecessary, the government nevertheless, had to pay for them.

The cost of passenger and freight travel became another point of conflict between the railroads and the public. Initially the railroads had charged low rates to carry freight, and as a result, companies carrying freight by wagon or boat were driven out of business. With no competition, the railroads seized the opportunity to raise their shipping prices. As farmers realized that they were losing money because of inflated freight charges, they began burning their corn as fuel to heat their homes. The cry of "Raise less corn and more Hell"[46] became a protest slogan throughout the farming states.

In addition to the steep increases in shipping costs, the railroads also controlled the warehouses in which farmers stored their crops and charged extremely high prices for the service, knowing that

The railroads charged extremely high prices to hold cattle in pens before they were shipped by train to slaughterhouses.

THE GRANGE MOVEMENT

As the Great Plains began to fill with thousands of new farms, the agricultural industry in America experienced dramatic changes. Farmers needed to produce more food more efficiently to feed America's rapidly expanding population. As farmers turned toward industries for assistance, they soon found that they were spending more money than they were making. Banks charged high interest on farms and equipment loans, railroads raised their freight rates, and food brokers called "middlemen" bought grain and cattle from farmers and sold them to processing plants at great profits. Frustrated by these big businesses, farmers joined the Grange movement in record numbers to try to avoid losing their farms.

By the 1880s, more than eight hundred thousand farmers were members of the Grange movement, whose elected leaders began working with politicians to pass laws favorable to the farmers. The Grange leaders focused on the railroads more than any other industry because of the monopoly they enjoyed shipping farm products to metropolitan markets. The railroads made far more money shipping grain, vegetables, and cattle to processing factories than the farmers made producing them.

As a result of the Grange movement, small farmers were able to influence many state legislatures to enact what were known as the Granger laws. All of these laws succeeded in lowering railroad shipping rates, limiting interest rates on farm loans, and curtailing unfair middleman costs. In 1887, the U.S. government recognized the need to establish a state railroad commission to regulate the railroads.

The Grange movement gradually lost momentum, and by the beginning of the twentieth century, it was no longer an effective advocate for farmers. The significance of the Grange movement, however, is that for the first time in the history of American agriculture, farmers successfully organized against big businesses like the railroads to protect their livelihood.

the farmers had no alternative. The railroads applied this same practice to cattle pens along the rail lines in which cattle were held until being shipped to slaughterhouses.

DECEIVING THE IMMIGRANTS

American farmers were not the only ones who felt cheated by the railroads. Many foreigners who neither spoke English nor knew the geography and climate of the West purchased land that they later wished they had never seen.

The 12,800 acres given to the Union Pacific and Central Pacific for each mile of track they laid had great value to the railroads if they could sell the land. The problem, however, from the railroads' point of view was that the Homestead Act of 1862 had given away millions of acres of top-quality farmland to American citizens. Consequently, by the 1890s, most of the railroads were finding that the land the government had granted them was, on the whole, of little value.

The railroad agents who fanned out across Europe selling railroad land to would-be immigrants took advantage of many Europeans' lack of detailed knowledge about America. Their pamphlets and flashy brochures were distributed throughout major European cities. In 1870, the Union Pacific alone advertised in more than two thousand European newspapers and magazines. The brochures usually exaggerated the beauty of the land as well as its crop-growing potential. One Union Pacific brochure, for example, described the

Platte Valley, where fierce storms had stopped construction on the transcontinental railroad during the winters, as "a flowery meadow of great fertility clothed in nutritious grasses and watered by numerous streams."[47] Overestimation of rainfall and underestimation of winter temperatures were all part of the game to lure unsuspecting foreigners to buy poor-quality land. If individuals agreed to a sale in Europe and made a down payment, the railroads promised free passage to their new land once they reached New York.

These sales campaigns were extremely successful in luring unsuspecting immigrants to some of the least inviting territory in America. The Northern Pacific Railroad, for example, named the largest city in the territory, Bismarck, after the German chancellor Otto von Bismarck, who they falsely claimed had invested in the region. The Northern Pacific made this claim in hopes of attracting German immigrants to the region.

Upon their arrival at their destinations, many immigrants, realizing that they had been swindled, demanded a refund of their money and a return ticket to New York. The railroads, however, refused such requests. Some immigrants packed their belongings and went home at their own expense, but others, with no money left, had no option but to remain and make the best of their predicament.

Those who stuck it out on the land had to work hard and band together for mutual support. Many families gathered to share the work of building homes and barns. They dug water wells, plowed and planted the land, and hoped for the best.

Poor-quality soil and severe living conditions made property purchased by many immigrants worthless.

Many other immigrants, however, found themselves unable to coax a living from the rocky, poor-quality soil. Eventually they abandoned their worthless property and departed for the cities in search of factory work. For many of these disappointed immigrants, the dream of a life of rural plenty ended in urban poverty. American historian Judith Clark reports:

Some immigrants fled to the nation's interior, where they broke up the prairie, built farm communities and planted an entire region in wheat, rye, oats and other crops. Others swelled the population of cities like New York, Boston, Chicago, and San Francisco. There, they placed enormous strain on municipal systems, causing tenements and ethnic ghettoes to mushroom almost overnight. These devolved into great, sprawling slums awash with sewage and prone to every imaginable health hazard, slums that brought the combined difficulties of poverty, illiteracy and disease to their unsuspecting inhabitants. It was this urban nightmare that, in turn, provoked the remarkable and ambitious reform efforts of this period.[48]

Thanks, however, to the efforts of those who stayed on the land to make the best of a broken dream, a vast wasteland was turned into productive farmland and ranches to feed the American people.

Mastering New Frontiers

From the very start, four hundred years ago, most of those arriving on America's shores saw the country as a new beginning or an escape from one sort of injustice or another. The uncharted frontier that spread westward beyond the Appalachians in the eighteenth century provided such opportunities. The vastness of the continent continued to provide new possibilities for nineteenth-century Americans who ventured first as far as the Mississippi River and then across it up to the Missouri River.

The transcontinental railroad opened the last geographical frontier, helping to populate it with the last of the American pioneers. As the rails crisscrossed America, the railroads continued the sense of newness for Americans by carrying them to new lives. The railroads helped Americans realize all of the opportunities that the nation's frontier still had to offer.

The beginning of the twentieth century, however, witnessed the closing of America's geographical frontier. The seemingly endless, unspoiled territory, earlier Americans had experienced had at last been exhausted. The transcontinental railroad, which contributed mightily to the opening of the frontier, also contributed to its closing as cities and towns peppered the landscape.

Americans correctly realized that the closing of geographical frontiers did not mean that all frontiers were gone. As Americans began to look for new frontiers to conquer in manufacturing, medicine, technology, and social reform, they also began to look for new and better means of transportation. By the 1940s, automobiles and trucks began to replace trains as the favored mode of transportation, and by the 1970s, airplanes further reduced America's interest in and dependence on the railroads.

Just as Americans found new, non-physical frontiers to conquer, they also found new forms of rail travel that would have astonished those who built the transcontinental railroad. Subways and light-rail systems now speed millions of commuters to work each day. Although such travel rarely affords the picturesque scenery that nineteenth-century travelers enjoyed, these railroads nonetheless, safely speed people wherever they want to go. As the twenty-first century opens, large metropolitan areas

The builders of the first Transcontinental Railroad would have been amazed by today's light-rail systems.

are being served by bullet trains capable of carrying passengers at speeds of up to two hundred miles an hour.

A still more revolutionary concept, Mag-Lev trains, promise even speedier and more reliable service. These trains will, by means of powerful magnets, levitate above the track without ever touching it. Mag-Lev trains are still in experimental stages, but they are expected to be capable of traveling twice the speed of bullet trains. Some transportation engineers believe that Mag-Lev trains may one day replace much of the world's dependence on airplanes.

As Americans continue to move forward further and further away from the time when the transcontinental railroad closed the physical frontier, new frontiers are being discovered that continue to provide fresh starts and new opportunities for future generations.

Notes

Chapter 1: America's Will: Manifest Destiny

1. Quoted in John M. Blum, *The National Experience*. New York: Harcourt Brace Jovanovich, 1989, p. 141.

2. Quoted in Carroll C. Calkins, ed., *The Story of America*. Pleasantville, NY: Reader's Digest Association, 1975, p. 71.

3. Quoted in *United States Magazine and Democratic Review*, July/August 1845.

4. Quoted in Blum, *The National Experience*, p. 255.

5. Quoted in Edward S. Barnard, *The Story of the Great American West*. Pleasantville, NY: Reader's Digest Association, 1977, p. 145.

Chapter 2: America's Ability: The Industrial Revolution

6. Quoted in American Studies Website at the University of Virginia. http://xroads.virginia.edu.

7. Quoted in American Studies Website.

8. Oliver Evans, *The Abortion of the Young Steam Engineers Guide*, Article 1, "Of Steam." 1805. www.history.rochester.edu/steam/evans/1805/article1.html.

9. Evans, *Young Steam Engineers Guide*, Advertisements. 1805. www.history.rochester.edu/steam/evans/1805/advertisement.html

Chapter 3: Linking East and West

10. Quoted in John Hoyt Williams, *A Great and Shining Road: The Epic Story of the Transcontinental Railroad*. New York: Times Books, 1988, p. 9.

11. Quoted in Stephen E. Ambrose, *Nothing Like It in the World: The Men Who Built the Transcontinental Railroad, 1863–1869*. New York: Simon and Schuster, 2000, p. 26.

12. Quoted in Calkins, *The Story of America*. p. 77.

13. Quoted in Williams, *A Great and Shining Road*, p. 15.

14. Quoted in George Kraus, *High Road to Promontory: Building the Central Pacific (now the Southern Pacific) Across the High Sierra*. Palo Alto, CA: American West Publishing, 1969, p. 13.

15. Quoted in Dee Brown, *Hear That Lonesome Whistle Blow: Railroads in the West*. New York: Touchstone, 1977, p. 48.

16. Quoted in Ambrose, *Nothing Like It in the World*, p. 33.

Chapter 4: The Central Pacific: East Across the Sierra Nevada

17. Quoted in Wesley S. Griswald, *A Work of Giants: Building the First Transcontinental Railroad*. New York: McGraw-Hill, 1962, p. 39.

18. Quoted in Ambrose, *Nothing Like It in the World*, pp. 108-109.

19. *Daily Alta Californian*, May 1, 1869.

20. Quoted in Ben Maddow, *A Sunday Between Wars: The Course of American Life from 1865 to 1917*. New York: W. W. Norton, 1979, p. 59.

21. Ambrose, *Nothing Like It in the World*, p. 194.

22. Quoted in Ambrose, *Nothing Like It in the World*, p. 195.

23. Quoted in Ambrose, *Nothing Like It in the World*, p. 247.

Chapter 5: The Union Pacific: West Across the Great Plains

24. Henry Morton Stanley, *The Autobiography of Sir Henry Morton Stanley*. Boston: Houghton Mifflin, 1909, p. 129.

25. Quoted in Ambrose, *Nothing Like It in the World*, p. 130.

26. Stanley, *Autobiography*, p. 226.

27. Quoted in Williams, *A Great and Shining Road*, p. 140.

28. Quoted in Williams, *A Great and Shining Road*, p. 198.

29. Quoted in Williams, *A Great and Shining Road*, p. 198.

30. Quoted in Judith Freeman Clark, *America's Gilded Age*. New York: Facts On File, 1992, p. 25.

31. Grenville M. Dodge, *How We Built the Union Pacific Railroad*. Council Bluffs, IA: Monarch Printing, 1997, p. 22.

32. Quoted in John Debo Galloway, *The First Transcontinental Railroad*, New York: Simmons-Boardsman, 1950, p. 232.

33. *Daily Alta Californian*, May 10, 1869.

Chapter 6: The Race to Settle the New American Landscape

34. Clark, *America's Gilded Age*, p. xv.

Chapter 7: Troubling Consequences

35. Quoted in Clark, *America's Gilded Age*, p. 93.

36. Quoted in Barnard, *The Story of the Great American West*, p. 268.

37. Quoted in Maddow, *A Sunday Between Wars*, p. 43.

38. Quoted in Brown, *Hear That Lonesome Whistle Blow*, p. 184.

39. Quoted in Brown, *Hear That Lonesome Whistle Blow*, p. 185.

40. Maddow, *A Sunday Between Wars*, p. 69.

41. Quoted in Ambrose, *Nothing Like It in the World*, p. 320.

42. Ambrose, *Nothing Like It in the World*, p. 320.

43. Henry David Thoreau, *Walden*. New York: Libra, 1960, p. 37.

44. Quoted in Ambrose, *Nothing Like It in the World*, p. 376.

45. Ambrose, *Nothing Like It in the World*, p. 376.

46. Brown, *Hear That Lonesome Whistle Blow*, p. 279.

47. Marilyn Miller, *The Transcontinental Railroad*. Cincinnati, OH: Silver Burdett, 1986, p. 55.

48. Clark, *America's Gilded Age*, p. xv.

For Further Reading

Books

Stephen E. Ambrose, *Nothing Like It in the World: The Men Who Built the Transcontinental Railroad, 1863–1869*. New York: Simon and Schuster, 2000. Focuses on the construction of the transcontinental railroad as well as the politics and funding that made it a reality.

Carroll C. Calkins, ed., *The Story of America*. Pleasantville, NY: Reader's Digest Association, 1975. A general American history book from the founding of America to the present. It presents a chronology of major American history themes and presents good explanations of cause and effect. The book is liberally peppered with photographs, quotations, and art representing the many themes of American history.

Judith Freeman Clark, *America's Gilded Age*. New York: Facts On File, 1992. Clark's book covers the last half of nineteenth-century American history. She investigates the American excess, including the transcontinental railroad, that resulted from the success of America's industrial revolution. Each chapter opens with an insightful analysis, followed by a broad selection of quotations and a list of factual events.

David Colbert, ed., *Eyewitness to the American West*. New York: Penguin Books, 1998. An excellent collection of eyewitness accounts of the events shaping the history of the American West. It contains 154 citations describing major events in chronological order. Each citation is briefly described to set its time and importance.

John Debo Galloway, *The First Transcontinental Railroad*. New York: Simmons-Boardsman, 1950. Galloway's book is a wonderful compendium of statistics and quotations that describe the difficulties of building two thousand miles of rail across the western United States. This book provides one of the best technical descriptions of the construction of trestles and roadbeds along the Sierra Nevada.

Wesley S. Griswald, *A Work of Giants: Building the First Transcontinental Railroad*. New York: McGraw-Hill, 1962. Griswald's work on the transcontinental railroad focuses exclusively on the engineering issues that the Central Pacific and Union Pacific faced as they worked their way across the continent. The book has a good selection of photographs and interesting insights into the major railroad figures.

George Kraus, *High Road to Promontory: Building the Central Pacific (now the Southern Pacific) Across the High Sierra*. Palo Alto, CA: American West Publishing, 1969. One of the best books describing the work of the Central

Pacific over the Sierra Nevada. The story is complete and the style fun to read. The book has wonderful photographs to elucidate the difficulties of construction over and through the granite mountains.

Marilyn Miller, *The Transcontinental Railroad*. Cincinnati, OH: Silver Burdett, 1986. An excellent, easy-to-read book, well documented with period photographs.

Henry Morton Stanley, *The Autobiography of Sir Henry Morton Stanley*. Boston: Houghton Mifflin, 1909. An excellent account of the life of this famed British traveler. In it, Stanley recounts many of his most memorable experiences traveling in America before and during the building of the transcontinental railroad. Of the many firsthand accounts of the American West during the mid–nineteenth century, this is one of the most intriguing.

John Hoyt Williams, *A Great and Shining Road: The Epic Story of the Transcontinental Railroad*. New York: Times Books, 1988. This book has an excellent account of the construction of the transcontinental railroad as well as some of the social problems created by it. Williams exposes the corruption of the railroads, obstacles to the Chinese living in California, and the questionable alliance between the railroads and the government.

Websites

Internet History Sourcebooks Project, (www.fordham.edu/halsall/). This website, presented by Fordham University, provides an excellent collection of primary source material.

Works Consulted

Books

John Bakeless, *The Eyes of Discovery: America as Seen by the First Explorers*. New York: Dover, 1961. Firsthand observations of several explorers of the New World, some famous and some lesser-known. The accounts contain interesting chronicles of first encounters with people, animals, and plants in the Americas.

Edward S. Barnard, *The Story of the Great American West*. Pleasantville, NY: Reader's Digest Association, 1977. This book covers the American West as it expanded from the Appalachian Mountains to the Pacific. It provides excellent insights into cultural differences of indigenous peoples. Excellent artwork.

John M. Blum, *The National Experience*. New York: Harcourt Brace Jovanovich, 1989. This large work spans the entire history of the United States. It highlights all major historical and cultural movements, as well as the people who were involved and responsible. Also provides an excellent selection of quotations from the nation's leaders.

Dee Brown, *Hear That Lonesome Whistle Blow: Railroads in the West*. New York: Touchstone, 1977. Dee Brown's book is a study in the construction of the railroad as well as the corruption that followed. Unlike most books discussing the history of the transcontinental railroad, Brown correctly investigates the impact of the railroad on immigrants, farmers, and other groups that suffered at the hands of the railroads.

Dennis Karwatka, *Technology's Past: America's Industrial Revolution and the People Who Delivered the Goods*. Ann Arbor, MI: Prakken Publications, 1996. This book is a collection of seventy-seven significant American inventors, spanning the period from the colonial era to the present. A brief biography of each inventor is provided, along with the significance of the invention(s) and a good description of the invention, including drawings and photographs.

Ben Maddow, *A Sunday Between Wars: The Course of American Life from 1865 to 1917*. New York: W. W. Norton, 1979. Maddow's book focuses on the period of American history from the end of the Civil War to the end of World War I. Maddow does not focus on the transcontinental railroad but rather paints a general picture of American society evolving from the Civil War and the expansion of America. The railroad is a major topic, as is the impact it had on all segments of the American population. Maddow devotes much of his book to the role of immigrants in America and the role the working class played in America's emergence as a world power at the beginning of the twentieth century.

Salvadore A. Ramirez, *The Octopus Speaks: The Colton Letters*. Carlsbad, CA: Tentacled Press, 1982. This book is a collection of letters written by the Big Four of the Central Pacific Railroad during the course of the construction of the transcontinental railroad. Its fascination and value lies with the many comments made regarding questionable business practices in which the four men engaged. These letters, meant to remain private, exist in the public record today as a result of a lawsuit in which they were admitted into evidence. They make for fascinating reading.

Henry David Thoreau, *Walden*. New York: Libra, 1960. Thoreau's most famous literary work, this is a journal of the author's thoughts and observations made while living for two years in an isolated cabin at Walden Pond.

Walt Whitman, *Passage to India*. New York: Viking Portable Library, 1965. This poem employs trains and sailing ships as symbols of Whitman's vision for bridging the East and West.

Periodicals

United States Magazine and Democratic Review, July/August 1845.

Wild West, "Lakota Noon at the Greasy Grass," June 1996.

Websites

American Studies program, University of Virginia (http://xroads.virginia.edu).

Department of History, University of Rochester (www.history.rochester.edu).

Index

Adams, Charles Francis, 104

advertisements, 44—45, 87, 109

agriculture. *See* farmers

Ambrose, Stephen, 105

America's Bread Basket, 91

Ames, Oakes, 104

Appalachian Mountains, 13

Arapaho, 72

Austin, Moses and Steven, 21

avalanches, 63

Baltimore and Ohio Railroad, 36

Barnard, Henry, 30

Big Four, 46–47, 53–54, 105

see also Crocker, Charles; Hopkins, Mark; Huntington, Collis; Stanford, Leland

Black Goose, 63–65, 68

Boone, Daniel, 13

Boot Hill, 96

Bozeman Trail, 77

Britain

Appalachian territory and, 13–14

industrial revolution in, 29, 31

Oregon and, 21

railroads in, 36, 38

brothels, 75

buffalo, 96, 98–100

bullet trains, 113

Burnettizer, 76

California

Mexico and, 20–21

natural resources of, 21

Sierra Nevada and, 21–22

travel to

dangers of, 41

routes for, 10, 22–24

canals, 27–29

cannibalism, 41

Cape Horn (Sierra Nevada), 61

Cape Horn (South America), 10, 24–25, 86

Casement, Dan, 71

Casement, John, 71, 75

Casement Army, 71

Central Overland California and Pikes Peak Express Company, 43

Central Pacific Railroad

construction costs and, 54, 68

financing of, 48, 51

formation of, 45, 47

labor needs of, 55–56

Chinese immigrants and, 54–58

Civil War veterans and, 71

Irish immigrants and, 71

Mormons and, 81

materials used, 68

profits and, 66

route of, 54, 80-82

dangers of, 61, 63

track-laying competitions and, 67, 69, 81

Truckee Valley line and, 65, 68

see also transcontinental railroad

Cherokee, 19

Cheyenne, 72, 78, 80

children

education of, 30

in factories, 34

Chinese immigrants

Central Pacific Railroad and, 56–58, 61, 67, 68

Chinese Exclusion Act and, 106

diet of, 64

track-laying competitions and, 67, 68, 81

cities, 90–91
Civil War
    hobos and, 94
    labor shortage caused
        by, 51, 70
    transcontinental
        railroad and
        need for, 47
    route of, 44
    veterans, 70, 79
Clark, Judith
    on immigrants
        importance of, 87–88
        life in United States,
            110–11
Clark, William, 16, 17
Clermont (steamboat), 345
Cleveland, Grover, 91
Clipper Gap, 59
coaches, 26, 83, 86
colonies, 13
Commager, Henry
    Steele, 105
Conestoga wagons, 27
cottonwoods, 75
Council Bluffs, Iowa, 47
Crazy Horse, 102
Crédit Mobilier, 103–105
Crocker, Charles
    background of, 45–47
    on Chinese immigrant
        laborers, 56–58
    Irish immigrants and,
        56
    track-laying
        competitions and, 65,
            67–68

Truckee Valley line
    and, 65
Tunnel Number 6 and,
    62
see also Big Four
Cumberland Gap, 13
Cumberland Road, 27
Cushing, Caleb, 20
Custer, George
    Armstrong, 102

Daily Alta California
    (newspaper), 56
Dana, Richard Henry, 21
Davis, Jefferson, 42–44
Deere, John, 32, 92
Dey, Peter, 50, 70
Dodge, Grenville
    background of, 50, 70
    on Dey, 50
    on Native Americans
        attacks by, 79
        campaign against,
            72–73
    on route through
        Rocky Mountains,
        80, 81
Dodge City, Kansas, 96,
    97
Donner Party, 41
Durant, Thomas C.
    Burnettized wood and,
        76
    chief engineer and, 50
    Crédit Mobilier and,
        104–105
    Railroad Act of 1864

and, 51
track-laying
    competitions and, 67,
        68–69
Dutch Flats, 61

education, 30
England
    Appalachian territory
        and, 13–14
    industrial revolution
        in, 29, 31
    Oregon and, 21
    railroads in, 36, 38
Erie Canal, 28–29
Evans, Oliver, 31

factories, 33–35, 88
see also industrial
    revolution
farmers
    America's Bread
        Basket and, 91
    Grange movement
        and, 108
    immigrants as, 86
    importance of to
        Jefferson, 14
    machinery for, 32–33,
        92
    railroads and, 12,
        92–93, 107–109
    Sod Busters, 92
Fetterman, William, 79
food, 64
Fort Dodge, 96
forts, 77–78

gambling, 75
gold, 21, 47, 56, 102
golden spike, 83, 84
Governor Stanford
  (locomotive), 52
graders, 73–74
Grange movement, 108
Grant, Ulysses S., 73, 88
Great American Desert,
  10, 39, 81, 88–90, 91
Great Depression, 94
Great Plains
  names for, 38
  Native Americans and
    attacks on Union
    Pacific Railroad
    crews, 72–73
  buffalo and, 98
  Homestead Act of
    1862 and, 88–89
  travel across, 10
Great Void, 39

Hall, Margaret, 27
Hanson-Stone, JoAnn, 89
Hell on Wheels, 75
hobos, 94
Homestead Act of 1862,
  48, 88–89, 109
Hopkins, Mark
  background of, 44–47
  on completion of
    Tunnel Number 6, 68
  see also Big Four
Hunt, Walter, 33
Huntington, Collis
  background of, 46–47

groundbreaking
  ceremony and, 52
  Railroad Act of 1864
  and, 51
  see also Big Four

immigrants
  Chinese
    Central Pacific
      Railroad and,
      56–58, 67, 68
    Chinese Exclusion
      Act and, 106
    diet of, 64
    in cities, 110–11
    education and, 30
    in factories, 34
    importance of, 87–88
  Irish
    Central Pacific
      Railroad and, 56
    diet of, 64
    Union Pacific
      Railroad and, 64,
      67
  land ownership and,
    41–42
  transcontinental
    railroad
    advertisements and,
    87, 109
  westward expansion
    and, 11, 88
  women, 89
Indian Removal Act
  (1830), 18, 19
Indian Territory, 18, 43

industrial revolution
  in Britain, 29, 31
  development of, 31–35
  education and, 30
  farmers and, 92
  railroads and, 92–93
    rails for, 49–50
  transcontinental, 86
Iron Horse, 72
Isthmus of Panama, 10,
  23–24, 86

Jefferson, Thomas
  Cumberland Road and,
    27
  on farmers, 14
  Lewis and Clark
    expedition and, 16,
    17
John Deere Company, 32
Johnson, Andrew, 80, 100
Judah, Theodore
  background of, 44–45
  Big Four and, 45–47,
    53–54
  death of, 54
  formation of Central
    Pacific Railroad and,
    45, 47
  on manifest destiny,
    44–45
  objective of, 53
  route and, 52, 54–55

Keseberg, Lewis, 41

laborers

Chinese immigrants,
56–58, 58, 67, 68
Civil War veterans, 71,
79
dangers to, 61–63
Irish immigrants, 56,
67
Mormons, 81–82
need for, 50–51
number of, 60
Pullman Company
and, 91
shortage of, 51, 55–57,
70
train crews, 103, 104
land ownership
colonists and, 13
Homestead Act of 1862
and, 48
immigrants and, 41–42,
109
importance of, to
Americans, 14–15
value of grants to
railroads, 48–49, 105,
109
see also Native
Americans, land
ownership and
Lewis, Meriwether, 16,
17
light-rail systems, 112
Lincoln, Abraham, 45, 48
Little Bighorn, Battle of
the, 102
locomotives
Black Goose, 63–65, 68

cost of, 52, 68
early, 36
improvements in, 38
Lorillard, Pierre, 32
Los Angeles, 106
Louisiana Purchase,
15–17
Low, Frederick F., 56
Lowell Mill Girls
(Robinson), 34
Lyceum, 30

Maddow, Ben, 100, 101
Mag-Lev trains, 113
mail, 43, 83, 86
manifest destiny
California and, 21
closing of frontier and,
95–96, 112
described, 18–21
Great American Desert
and, 81
Louisiana Purchase
and, 16
transcontinental
railroad and, 39–40,
44–45
Mann, Horace, 30
Marshall, John, 19
Martineau, Harriet,
14–15
May, John, 15
McCormick, Cyrus,
32–33, 92
meals, 64, 67
Mexican-American War,
85

Mexico, 20–21, 85
milling industry, 31
minerals, 48–49, 51
mines, 95
M&M Railroad, 70
Morison, Samuel Eliot,
105
Mormons, 81–82
Morris, Isaac, 101

National Road, 27
Native Americans
attacks by, 10, 39
on Central Pacific
Railroad, 72–73
in Ohio Valley, 15
on Soo Line, 102
on Union Pacific
Railroad, 78–80
land ownership and
concept of, 17, 98
Railroad Act of 1862
and, 47
Railroad Act of 1864
and, 51
treaties and, 19
Union Pacific
Railroad and,
72–73, 78–80
negotiations with, 80
removal of, 18, 19
transcontinental
railroad and, 12
treaties with, 17
natural resources
in California, 21
Homestead Act of 1862

and, 48
industrial revolution
    and, 85
Railroad Act of 1862
    and, 48
nitroglycerin ("nitro"), 63
Northern Pacific
    Railroad, 109

Ohio Valley, 15
One-eyed Boss Man, 58
Oregon, 21

"Pacific Railroad Ring,
    The" (Adams), 104
packet boats, 28–29
Panama, 10, 22–24, 86
Parker, Ely S., 99
Philadelphia (passenger
    Steamer), 24
poker, 75
Pony Express, 43
Poor, Henry
    on Great Void, 39
    on importance of
        transcontinental
        railroad, 40
*Poor's Manual of Railroads
    of the United States*
    (Poor), 40
population
    before eighteenth
        century, 13
    growth of, 41, 88
Promontory
    Summit/Point, 69,
    82–84

Pullman, George, 91
Pullman Palace Car
    Company, 91

race riots, 106
Railroad Act of 1862
    amendment to, 65–66
    building specifications
        of, 49–50, 59, 70
    land ownership and,
        47, 48
    route and, 47, 65
Railroad Act of 1864, 51
railroads
    accidents on, 97, 101
    advertisements for, 109
    early, 35–37
    in eastern United
        States, 40
    farmers and, 92–93,
        107–109
    importance of, 35–36
    industrial revolution
        and, 31
    mines and, 95
    modern, 112–113
    public opinion about,
        105
    ranchers and, 93–95
    shipping costs on,
        37–38
    specialized cars, 60, 91,
        92–93, 95
    see also transcontinental
        railroad
railroad towns, 90–91
rails

cost of, 68, 76
    improvements in, 38
    incline of, 49, 59–61
    laying of, 74–76, 81
        competitions, 67, 68,
        81
    shortage of, 68
ranchers, 12, 93–95
reapers, 32–33
Rensselaer Polytechnic
    Institute, 30
reservations, 100
roads, 25–26
Robinson, Harriet
    Hanson, 34
Rock Springs, Wyoming,
    106
Rocky Mountains, 39,
    80–81

Sacramento, California,
    44, 47
Sacramento Railroad, 44
saloons, 75
Santa Fe Trail, 92
scalping, 78
schools, 30
Shannon, Fred, 105
Sherman, William
    Tecumseh, 76–77
Sherman Summit, 81
Sierra Nevada
    Cape Horn, 61–62
    Central Pacific Railroad
        route and, 53
    Clipper Gap, 59
    dangers of, 10, 39

described, 21

Donner Party and, 41

expense of laying track
over, 65

travel to California
and, 21–22

Tunnel Number 6,
62–63, 65

weather in, 63

Sioux, 72, 75, 77, 98

Sitting Bull, 102

Slater, Samuel, 33

Sod Busters, 92

Soo Line, 102

spikers, 76

stagecoaches, 27, 83, 86

Stanford, Leland
background of, 45–47
completion of
transcontinental
railroad and,83 , 84
see also Big Four

Stanley, Henry Morton
on Native Americans
attacks by, 72
land ownership and,
73
scalping by, 78

steamboats, 35, 42–44

steam engines, 29, 31, 35

Stevens, Robert L., 38

St. Joseph, Missouri, 43

Strobridge, Jim
Chinese immigrants
and, 57–58, 61
described, 58
Tunnel Number 6 and, 65

subways, 112

Sullivan, John L., 19

Summit Tunnel, 62

Sunday Between Wars, A
(Maddow), 100, 101

surveyors, 73

tampers, 76

tea, 64

telegraph company, 78

Texas, 21

textiles, 31, 33–34

Thompson, William, 78

Thoreau, Henry David, 105

tobacco, 32

Tombstone, 97

tools, 60, 63

tourism, 96, 99

transcontinental railroad
closing of frontier and,
112
completion of, 83–84
cost of travel on, 86
expansion of, 88,
103–107
industrial revolution
and, 85
opposition to, 42–44,
105
reasons for, 85–86
route of, 42, 44, 47, 68
westward expansion
and, 10, 11, 39–40,
44–45, 77, 80, 81, 94
see also Central Pacific
Railroad; railroads;
Union Pacific

Railroad
Truckee Valley line, 65, 66

Tunnel Number 6, 58,
62–63, 65

Two Years Before the Mast
(Dana), 21

Union Pacific Railroad
advertisements by, 109
attacks by Native
Americans on, 76–78
chief engineer for, 50
Crédit Mobilier and,
103–105
crews of, 73–76
financing of, 48, 50, 51,
76
labor needs of, 50–51, 61
Mormons and, 81–82
profits from, 81
Railroad Act of 1862
and, 70
route of, 73
shoddy construction
and, 101
surveying crews of, 65
track-laying
competitions and, 67,
68, 81
see also transcontinental
railroad

U.S. Army
Battle of the Little
Bighorn and, 102
Corps of Engineers, 42

U.S. Congress
transcontinental

railroad and
financing of, 42, 51
opposition to, 42–43
route for, 42, 44
see also Railroad Acts
universities, 30

Vanderbilt, Cornelius, 54
Vincennes Western Sun
(newspaper), 42

Washington, George, 27
weather, 63
Webster, Daniel, 42

Wells, David, 92–93
West Point, 30
westward expansion,
80–81
closing of frontier and,
95–97, 112
in eighteenth century, 13
Louisiana Purchase
and, 15–17
Native Americans and
removal of, 18, 19
treaties with, 17
transcontinental railroad
and, 10, 11, 39–40,

44–45, 72, 78–79
see also manifest
destiny
whiskey, 75
Whitney, Eli, 32, 34–35
women, 34, 89
wood
amount used, 10–11
Burnettized, 76
cost of, 76
shortage of, 74–76, 81
workers. *See* laborers

Young, Brigham, 81–82

Picture Credits

Cover photo: Hulton Getty Collection

Archive Photos, 16, 66 (right), 85

© Morton Beebe, S.F./CORBIS, 113

© Bettmann/CORBIS, 18, 20, 22, 24, 26, 33, 35, 50, 66 (left), 71, 82, 104, 107, 110

© CORBIS, 59, 83, 90

© Jay Dickman/CORBIS, 14

© Hulton-Deutsch Collection/CORBIS, 62

Library of Congress, 36, 37, 42, 57, 72, 74, 77, 87, 99

© Medford Historical Society Collection/CORBIS, 49, 103

© Minnesota Historical Society/CORBIS, 93

© David Muench/CORBIS, 28, 40, 53

North Wind Picture Archives, 55, 60

© Lee Snider; Lee Snider/CORBIS, 29

© Oscar White/CORBIS, 70

About the Author

James Barter received his undergraduate degree in history and classics at the University of California (Berkeley), followed by graduate studies in ancient history and archaeology at the University of Pennsylvania. Mr. Barter has taught history as well as Latin and Greek. A Fulbright scholar at the American Academy in Rome, Mr. Barter worked on archaeological sites in and around the city as well as on sites in the Naples area. Mr. Barter has also worked and traveled extensively in Greece.

Mr. Barter currently lives in Rancho Santa Fe, California, with his fifteen-year-old daughter, Kalista, who enjoys soccer, piano, and mathematics. Mr. Barter's older daughter, Tiffany Modell, lives in Kansas City where she plays violin with the Kansas City Symphony.